The Simple Guide To Budgeting

"Master Your Finance With Practical
Tips And Proven Strategies"

Joseph L. Wolford

The Simple Guide To Budgeting

You are solely responsible for any consequences that may result from putting such information to use. Before making any financial decisions or implementing any financial strategies discussed in this book, you should seek advice from a qualified financial professional.

The Simple Guide To Budgeting

Table Of Content

The Simple Guide To Budgeting

INTRODUCTION

Inside the dynamic panorama of personal finance, learning the art of budgeting is a cornerstone for reaching economic nicely-being. "A simple guide to Budgeting" serves as your compass in navigating the tricky world of managing cash wisely. A long way from a daunting assignment, budgeting is an empowering ability that empowers people to manipulate their financial destinies.

In the following pages, we will resolve the standards that shape the bedrock of effective budgeting, that specialize in 3 pivotal elements: the sensitive stability that underlies financial fulfillment, a comprehensive budgeting checklist to streamline your financial adventure, and the strategic integration of investing for a wealthy destiny.

Budgeting, at its essence, is more than mere quantity-crunching; it's far a holistic approach to aligning your monetary sources together with your existence dreams. As we embark on this journey together, we are able to demystify the complexities surrounding budgeting, offering you with realistic insights and actionable steps to construct a comfy and thriving financial foundation.

Whether you're simply starting your monetary adventure or searching to refine your existing budgeting practices, this manual is crafted to be accessible, informative, and relevant to a diverse range of monetary conditions. The aim is easy but profound: to empower you with the understanding and tools needed to make knowledgeable monetary choices, obtain stability to your economic life, and pave the way for a wealthy and gratifying future.

Get geared up to embark on a transformative exploration of budgeting—one which is going beyond numbers and charts to domesticate a mindset that ends in monetary success. Let's dive into the arena of "A simple manual to Budgeting" and release the keys to an extra at ease and rewarding financial destiny.

Definition of Budgeting

A Budget is a calculation plan, normally but not continually economic, for a defined duration, often three hundred and sixty five days or a month. A budget may additionally consist of predicted income volumes and revenues, aid portions which include time, prices and costs, environmental influences including greenhouse fuel emissions, other influences, assets, liabilities and coins flows. agencies, governments, families, and different companies use budgets to specific strategic plans of activities in measurable terms.

A finances expresses mean prices along with proposals for how to meet them with sources. A finances may additionally express a surplus, imparting resources to be used at a destiny time, or a deficit wherein expenditures exceed income or other resources.

Budgeting is finished via individuals, families, corporations, corporations, and the government—to plan, display, and control price range. it's far everywhere; homemakers use it to manipulate their monthly fees

and savings; the government is based on it to run the country.

anticipated revenue

and expected expenditure are the two vital components. anticipated sales is the potential cash inflow that someone, enterprise entity, or authorities would possibly generate. However, expected expenditure is the coin outflow that a person, company, or government expects to make in the upcoming period.

Budgets can be of two kinds – static and bendy. A static budget stays unchanged over the existence of the budget. regardless of the modifications at some stage in the budgeting length, at the start calculated money owed and figures remain the equal. Conversely, a bendy budget has relational price to positive variables.

A drastic change in variables influences the general budget. Each budget type is beneficial to control.

A static finances gauges the usefulness of the original price range, and a flexible budget offers sensible insights into commercial enterprise operations.

Importance of Budgeting in Personal Finance

Why Is Budgeting Crucial In Personal Finance management? Budgeting is a mighty tool that allows you to decide wherein you need to spend your money and how much you can spend. With a price range, you could ensure that each single rupee that you have earned is being used the way you want it and reveal your progress. Let us check the four motives why making plans and budgeting is vital even as making plans your non-public price range

1. Budgeting helps keep away from Overspending: your money haphazardly can result in spending greater than you ought to, mainly if you use any credit card or credit score programs. This may unavoidably lessen your spending power within the future, as most of your income will move into debt payments. Via developing finances on your monthly costs, you may be able to see how much you make vs how much you spend every month and can be in a higher function to identify whilst you must prevent spending.

2. Budgeting enables You reap Your monetary desires. A price range will assist you in recognizing how to save your money for your economic goals. These should consist of saving on your ideal property, setting up a training fund for your baby, beginning your very own commercial enterprise, and so forth. With finances, you could assemble a plan for each objective and investigate it periodically.

3. Budgeting Makes Saving simpler whilst you follow a finances, you may designate a set amount/percentage of your profits for unique goals and may transfer this quantity to a financial savings or funding account every month. This way you will be less likely to use this quantity for any charges.

4. Budgeting facilitates You benefit from managing Budgeting locations on top of things of your finances. Having a monetary plan enables you to prioritize your costs, reveal your progress, and make changes on every occasion required. A finances is a splendid tool to be able to resource in establishing a legitimate monetary future.

Overview of the Three Key Components: Balance, Budgeting Checklist, and Investing

attaining financial well-being entails a sensitive interaction day-to-day. "An easy manual day-to-day Budgeting" places a spotlight on three fundamental components that lay the inspiration for sound monetary control—balance, Budgeting checklist, and making an investment.

1. balance is key

monetary fulfillment is akin to a nicely-tuned orchestra, in which each tool plays a crucial role in creating concord. The primary aspect, "stability is fundamental," explores the art of reaching equilibrium to your economic lifestyles. From knowing the delicate balance between earnings and costs everyday establishing emergency funds and navigating the terrain of brief-time period versus long-time period goals, this section provides insights into growing stability and resilience within the face of lifestyles's monetary uncertainties.

2. Budgeting Checklist

Crafting an effective price range is extra than just allocating numbers; it is a strategic process that requires conscious attention and planning. The "Budgeting tick list" phase equips you with the gear and information needed to create a customized budget that aligns with your monetary targets. From assessing your profits and categorizing expenses everyday, fending off commonplace budgeting pitfalls, this aspect serves as a realistic manual everyday turning your monetary desires into actionable plans.

3. investing for the future

Beyond the confines of day to day budgeting lies the world of making an investment—an effective daily for securing your economic future. "investing for destiny" introduces to you daily the world of investment, losing its blessings, one of a kind motors day-to-day, and the mixing of investments in every day of your budget. Whether or not you're a beginner or seasoned investing day-to-day, this phase explores danger management, diversification, and the strategic allocation of funds day-to-day navigate the dynamic landscape of monetary markets.

Those 3 key additives form the core of our exploration, every gambling a pivotal function on your journey day-to-day monetary mastery. As we delve inday-to-day the intricacies of balance, the nuances of budgeting, and the strategic components of making an investment, you'll benefit from a complete know-how of day-to-day domestic financial resilience and make knowledgeable selections that make a contribution for your long-term prosperity. join us on this transformative day trip via "An easy guide every day Budgeting," in which monetary empowerment is within your attainment.

The Simple Guide To Budgeting

Chapter 1: Understanding the Basics

Definition and importance of budgeting

Budgeting is the process of putting a plan together to help you not only shop for money, but also recognize how to spend it. A price range can make sure you're not overspending and you could cover essential prices. It's regularly carried out monthly and you can re-evaluate it periodically.

In enterprise, budgeting works in a totally similar way. you can estimate precise revenue and any upcoming prices. This allows them to keep away from overspending and preserve cash waft in check. Budgeting may be used in my opinion and professionally. And it may be for an unmarried character, a business, or man or woman departments within an organization.

coping with month-to-month expenses correctly can make a big difference. It enables you to put together an unpredictable event or keep up for a large-price ticket object in the future. Preserving a budget can also make certain you don't take on any pointless debt.

without a budget, you can locate yourself with unexpected expenses. This can cause difficulty accomplishing business goals.

Importance of budgeting

Why is budgeting vital?

Budgeting isn't handiest useful for people who conflict financially. A price range is a stepping stone on your financial goals. It permits you to live inside your method and derive maximum blessings from to be had sources. Budgeting can assist as below:

1. financial cognizance: Budgeting helps to apprehend your courting with money. With finances, about your profits, spending scope, and saving opportunities. Normal tracking enables us to spot patterns and make modifications if required. In the long run, budgeting facilitates keeping away from frivolous prices and inculcates the economic field.

2. Emergencies: a really perfect price range earmarks finances for an emergency and plans for dreams like retirement or holiday. flexible budgets allow you to prepare allocation based totally on your immediate desires.

3. reduce Debt exposure: A budget lets you map out fees and reduces overspending. In effect, it limits or eliminates exposure to debt or credit score facilities.

4. Relieves pressure: Formulating a finances and adhering to it guarantees monetary independence. At the same time as budgeting isn't a remedy-all, it allows you to manipulate financial selections and put them together for demanding situations.

5. Reorganize expenses: Budgeting helps to forecast the ones months with tight finances and ones with greater liquidity. To make sure potential and clean budget, you could undertake techniques to even out the highs and lows in a price range.

6. purpose putting: A well-structured finances enables set possible goals. individuals can plan for fundamental lifestyles activities inclusive of buying a domestic or saving for retirement, while businesses can outline targets like increasing operations or launching new merchandise. Budgeting ensures that the essential budget is allotted closer to these desires, making them more conceivable.

7. selection Making: Budgets offer valuable insights that facilitate better choice-making strategies. With complete information on their financial situation, people could make smarter alternatives to investments or determine whether they could find the money for positive purchases.

Common misconceptions about budgeting

Depositing our pay cheques within the bank and the use of the credit and ATM card for spending seems easy. However, keeping track of your income and fees, to get full cost in your cash is feasible best with budgeting. Budgeting facilitates most of us to hold music of our earnings and spending and now not overspend. In exercise budgeting myths retard the savings of an entire life. they are:

1. I earn loads and need not price range:

This requires an exchange of angles. Michel Jackson lived like a king however died awash in $four hundred million debt. Budgeting by means of looking at your spending sample allows pointless charges on garments or eating out, and helps you shop for a destiny or for a much wanted dream excursion. So how much you earn has got much less relevance. What's extra important is budgeting. Right budgeting can make a low profits earner retire richer and overspending can make a high earnings earner a pauper.

2. I preserve a comfy task and spot no motive to keep:

this doesn't hold properly these days with large businesses getting into for exertions layoff to store fees during recession. Small groups also put you at a hazard with the loss of life of the proprietor or the enterprise going into losses. This insecurity demands caution to shop for spending at some point of such periods whilst you are caught unaware, with an emergency fund coming handy.

3. i'm negative in calculations and cannot finances:

With beneficial gear like spreadsheets that help account for charges and profits earned make budgeting tons easier .. A examine the spending enables avoid pointless expenses to finances and keep in future. In case you are involved, you'll be able to effortlessly examine budgeting. So in case you say 'I don't understand a way to make a budget', it indicates your stage of interest and willingness to keep for a secured destiny.

4. i'm fortunate; i will by no means be brief of cash:
but your ability in assembly, high payments and other unpredictable highly-priced events like existence threatening accidents, or a prime surgery without experiencing scarcity of money might not constantly be actual. So higher store and be organized to stand unpredicted contingencies after which use the savings for something else that you could take into account suitable.

5. I pay my bills right away and do no longer want budgeting:
Congratulations I appreciate your credit score worthiness, however going into poor stability is likewise quite easy. you may be self disciplined. It doesn't imply that you need not make a budget now. preparing finances makes you tons extra disciplined and spend consciously. So budgeting with savings facilitates keeping away from going into terrible balance or overdraft.

6. Budgeting may want to lead to deprivation: Budgeting isn't always frugal dwelling and foregoing all pleasures like a film a month and an devour out once a week, but it's miles simply now not allowing your earnings to be not overtaken with the aid of your fee. all and sundry is planning to store, planning to invest, however can we have a nicely idea out plan for spending. A smart spending plan can lead you to shop more. There's no need to feel deprived with budgeting; it is simply saving a percentage of your profits spent unnecessarily to have a secured future.

7. I have small desires and discover no want to keep:

This would not be a strong mindset in human nature, with you trying to take advantage of positive financial tendencies in the marketplace like buying residence or land at inexpensive quotes, or making an investment at higher costs towards building a bigger retirement corpus . For this reason budgeting enables you to save whilst you do not want cash for a time when you can profitably use it. Your wants can be small but simple needs like meals, safe haven, and garb are becoming more expensive with inflation. Also you need to keep in mind your fitness care wishes for destiny.

8. I am getting rises, bonus and tax refunds and discover no need to price range:

I think you have been fortunate most of these years, however those advantages are particularly unpredictable and setting one's hopes completely on them is futile. it's far higher to finance and save than depend on unpredictable blessings like bonus, improvement and tax refunds . The current recession has taught us a lesson to everybody which we must now not forget about without problems.

The impact of budgeting on financial well-being

Budgeting performs a vital function in shaping and improving monetary well-being. Financial well-being refers to a nation of universal monetary health, where people can meet their current monetary obligations, feel cozy about their financial future, and have the freedom to make selections that allow them to enjoy existence. here are several approaches wherein budgeting can affect economic properly-being:

Increased monetary management: Budgeting offers you a clear photo of your earnings and expenses, allowing you to song your spending habits and make knowledgeable economic selections. This ends in a sense of control and empowerment over your budget.

Reduced monetary pressure: Budgeting helps you control your cash effectively, that may extensively lessen financial pressure. knowing where your cash goes and having a plan for it could alleviate tension and worry about budget.

Progressed savings: Budgeting facilitates you to discover regions wherein you could reduce returns and allocate more resources in the direction of saving. This allows you to construct an emergency fund, store for destiny dreams, and attain monetary safety.

Reduced debt: via monitoring your fees and growing a spending plan, you may become aware of regions in which you're overspending and redirect the ones budget toward debt reimbursement. This facilitates you to pay down debt faster and improve your credit score rating.

Extended monetary literacy: The manner of making and preserving a budget encourages you to study personal finance and broaden healthful economic behavior. This elevated monetary literacy can empower you to make knowledgeable financial choices for the duration of your existence.

Stepped forward intellectual well-being: economic strain can negatively affect your intellectual fitness. Budgeting can help alleviate this stress, mainly to progress intellectual nicely-being and normal happiness.

More peace of mind: understanding that you have a plan for your finances can provide a sense of protection and peace of mind. This allows you to recognize other areas of your life without disturbing your monetary scenario.

The Simple Guide To Budgeting

Chapter 2: Developing a Healthy Money Mindset

Understanding the role of mindset in financial success.

One of the key factors that differentiate successful human beings from the rest is their fine mindset. Fine questioning permits you to overcome economically demanding situations and acquire your monetary desires. whilst you believe in yourself and your abilities, you are much more likely to do so in the direction of attaining your purpose

In relation to economic fulfillment, many human beings completely pay attention to monetary techniques and funding possibilities, frequently overlooking the essential role that attitude plays in this pursuit. The energy of mindset can't be underestimated, because it shapes our thoughts, ideals, and movements, in the end figuring out our level of achievement in wealth accumulation. In this phase, we will delve into the significance of mindset in achieving the preferred wealth effect, exploring distinctive views and supplying precious insights that will help you harness the energy of your mind-set.

1. The increased attitude: one of the most crucial mindsets to adopt whilst aiming for wealth creation is the growth mindset. Coined by psychologist Carol Dweck, the growth mind-set is the notion that intelligence, abilities, and abilities may be developed via determination and hard paintings. Embracing an increased mindset allows individuals to peer challenges as possibilities for growth and mastering, allowing them to persist through setbacks and in the long run acquire their financial desires. as an example, in preference to viewing a failed funding as a private failure, those with a boom mind-set might see it as a precious studying revel in and use it to make higher selections in the destiny.

2. The Abundance mind-set: any other effective attitude for attaining wealth is the abundance attitude. This mind-set is rooted in the belief that there's an unlimited delivery of opportunities, resources, and wealth to be had to every person. individuals with an abundance mind-set approach wealth introduction with a feel of optimism and gratitude, attracting more opportunities and economic abundance into their lives. As an example, in preference to viewing opposition as a chance, those with an abundance attitude see it as a threat to collaborate and create win-win situations, leading to more fulfillment in wealth accumulation.

3. The positive mindset: An effective mindset is vital in attaining the wealth impact as it impacts our thoughts, feelings, and actions. With the aid of retaining a tremendous outlook, individuals are much more likely to attract fulfillment and wealth into their lives. positive affirmations, visualization techniques, and gratitude practices are powerful equipment that could assist domesticate a high-quality mindset. For instance, regularly expressing gratitude for cutting-edge monetary benefits and envisioning future monetary success can significantly affect one's mind-set, leading to increased motivation and backbone in wealth-building endeavors.

4. The attitude of continuous learning: To reap the wealth impact, it's vital to undertake a mindset of non-stop mastering. Embracing a boom mindset and in search of possibilities to make bigger understanding and capabilities in the realm of wealth advent can result in sizable breakthroughs. This can involve reading books, attending seminars, networking with successful people, and staying up to date on the cutting-edge trends and strategies in finance and investment. With the aid of constantly getting to know and adapting, individuals could make informed choices and seize lucrative possibilities that contribute to their wealth accumulation.

5. The significance of mind-set shifting: ultimately, it's far essential to acknowledge that our attitude isn't fixed and can be shifted. spotting the want for mind-set shifts and consciously running towards converting proscribing beliefs and bad notion styles is critical for accomplishing the desired wealth impact. For instance, if a person has a scarcity mind-set, believing that there is by no means sufficient money to go round, they can work on shifting their mindset in the direction of abundance with the aid of reframing their mind and that specialize in possibilities for financial growth and prosperity.

information the power of attitude in accomplishing the wealth effect is paramount for those aiming to build wealth and financial independence. By adopting a growth mind-set, abundance mind-set, advantageous attitude, mindset of non-stop studying, and embracing attitude shifting, individuals can unlock their full potential and attract fulfillment of their wealth-building endeavors. recollect, wealth is not entirely determined by means of external factors but also by using the inner mindset and beliefs we preserve.

Tips and exercises to cultivate a positive money mindset.

Cash is an intricate subject matter. each person desires it to live on, but if you don't have sufficient of it, it can cause predominant strain. The shortage of money or the presence of too much debt can cause someone to broaden a terrible and unfavorable notion procedure in relation to finances. Once this way of questioning is instilled in a person's mind, it is able to affect their price range in methods the character might not even be privy to. If you constantly live in a nation of fear when it comes to cash, you may sabotage your chance of making more or getting out of debt. warding off considering your price range completely can cause you to dig yourself right into a deeper economic pit, that is why you want to shift your mind-set. Below, you'll find a few suggestions that will help you create a fine money mindset.

Forgive Your past economic mistakes

no person is perfect. possibilities are you've made multiple bad economic choices through the years. Perhaps you paid an excessive amount for the lease due to the fact you fell in love with a stunning house, otherwise you went on too many buying sprees, and now your credit score playing cards are maxed out. Some decisions you've made in the past are within the past. yes, you would possibly nonetheless be struggling with the outcomes of these mistakes, but you shouldn't continually beat yourself up over it. cash is difficult, and no longer everybody is taught a way to manipulate it nicely. loads of human beings find their way through trial and error. The 2 most essential things to consciousness are getting to know your errors and forgiving yourself.

You should additionally attempt to rephrase your wondering in relation to the terrible choices you've made inside the beyond. when you have debt, do not forget the dinners out with friends, recollect the journeys you took or the training you paid for. Your debt brought you joy, it created recollections. Don't romanticize it, but remember the fact that it served a motive. It's now not the enemy or a black void you'll in no way get out of. It became there whilst you needed it, and now you could work to pay it down and create an excellent better existence moving ahead.

Understand Your thoughts and emotions Surrounding cash

you would possibly think you recognize your concept patterns on the subject of cash, however taking a deeper appearance may provide a few exciting insights. try this workout: For a whole day, after each buy or financial choice you make, take a moment and write down your thoughts and emotions. What's going for walks through your head? How do you feel? Be sincere and thorough. On the rest of the day, go over the whole lot with open thoughts. you may locate that certain elements of your finances are stressing you out extra than you concept, or possibly a buy you notion could deliver you pleasure only brought fleeting happiness followed by guilt. You need to have no experience like you can't put money into yourself from time to time, but it's excellent to actually compare how your spending behavior is affecting your mental fitness, thoughts, and emotions.

Recognise That comparing yourself to Others is a dropping recreation

evaluating yourself to others is one of the most risky matters you may do in life, and the same is actually in the price range. Initially, comparisons are by no means accurate. The lens is skewed. Everything there is to know about yourself, but in case you're evaluating yourself to someone on Instagram, a movie megastar, or a fictional man or woman, you're actually evaluating yourself to someone you recognize almost nothing about. Social media is a lie. You best see what people want you to see. They publish the highlights of their lifestyles and monetary journey and omit the rest. for instance, you may see an Instagrammer posting about costly vacations, fancy clothes, and a lovely home, but you don't understand how much debt is on their credit score cards. You don't realize if they're two months behind on their car price or owe their mother and father hundreds of greenbacks. And also you'll by no means realize, due to the fact they gained a percentage of that part of their journey with you. but you constantly see the darker aspect of yours, so that you can see why evaluating your entire tale with the most effective highlight reel of theirs is dishonest and perilous.

Even if you're evaluating yourself to buddies or a circle of relatives members, you're nonetheless in a similar state of affairs. you may in no way Realize as much about them as you do approximately yourself, so that you can't completely recognize their economic scenario and the thoughts that move into tough selections. Every other downfall right here is that when you compare yourself and locate yourself on the losing end, you get discouraged. You're focusing on the bad as opposed to finding the wonderful. You start to see your dreams as unreachable. You are aware of your flaws in preference to how far you've come. minds like those can set you again and purpose you to make even extra bad monetary selections in the end.

work on Forming right habits
Don't shrink back from your price range. try, alternatively, to set aside time every week to go over your payments, finances, and spending habits. spotlight the regions you want to work on and congratulate yourself for any enhancements. Averting a problem will by no means make it depart. Instead, position your fears aside and face the problems head-on.

Set sensible desires and praise yourself in small ways while you reach them. Your price range didn't get out of hand overnight, and your success gained it appears in that manner both, so it's critical to set several small desires and celebrate each tremendous step.

Create a finances That Brings You joy
Budgets have a tendency to make people worried. They think of a budget as confining and restricting, however it doesn't necessarily be that way. An unfastened finances can help you live inside your spending parameters and recognize your obstacles at the same time as nonetheless allowing yourself the freedom to deal with yourself from time to time. A very good rule of thumb is to place half of your month-to-month earnings towards payments and requirements. Twenty percent of your earnings should be going in the direction of paying off debt or building savings. That leaves thirty percent as a way to use as you please. In case you discover that you're not able to comply with this sample, it is probably time to examine your monthly payments and notice which of them you may decrease or cut out altogether.

Bear in mind to be thankful

be thankful for the entirety you have; it might not be as plenty as you need, however it's what you have got right now, and it's worth celebrating. be pleased about the roof over your head, the task that offers you with earnings, the automobile that helps you get around, the food in your fridge, and many others. There's usually time in life to make extra cash and construct a higher existence, but it'll never be enough until you discover ways to focus on what you have got with a grateful heart.money shouldn't manage you or your mind. As an alternative, you have to work to govern your mind around cash and in turn begin to get a higher grip on your financial spending. Use these pointers to get you begun and watch as your thoughts and emotions on money begin to have a superb effect in your existence.

Overcoming common mindset barriers to budgeting.

Budgeting is the simplest tool for coping with your cash. It not most effectively indicates how you are spending your cash, however it also maintains you from falling into debt. The high-quality component? Following a price range does no longer suggest you need to give up the matters you adore maximum in existence. alternatively, having a budget in an area will shed light on what the ones activities are and what sort of importance you place upon them.

Why are such a lot of people averse to budgeting? Even as the records vary, an extensively quoted Gallup survey observed that the handiest 32% of yank families put together a written budget or use software for a spending plan. Some other surveys accomplished by using Bankrate found that fewer than 40% of Americans have cash for a $500 or $1,000 emergency. if you discover yourself aligning with either statistic, take a second and breathe

Here are six ways to change your mindset around budgeting.

1. Understand your 'tale.'

Take a moment to reflect on what comes up for you whilst you reflect on consideration of cash. Write down all of your money beliefs, irrespective of what they're. Perhaps you observed that you'll in no way get out of debt, or that at some point a person will magically pay it off for you. Perhaps you observed that cash is meant to be stored, not spent. Perhaps you suspect rich human beings are grasping, or that negative humans can't seize destruction. Whatever comes to mind, get it down on paper.

Now, check that list of statements you made. you could be surprised how a number of these beliefs got here in the first place. you may even find out preconceived notions you didn't realize you had. Now which you've introduced those thoughts to the forefront, you've got an idea of where you could evolve. decide which cash beliefs are well worth keeping, and which ones you could ditch.

You get to create your new money tale. What do you need it to seem like?

2. go from fixed mind-set to growth mindset.

let's maintain it simple and expect there are mindsets: constant and growth. One will keep you back, whereas the other will enable you to create trade. A boom mindset goes an extended manner on the subject of placing and preserving your budget.

have you ever ever stuck your self saying "I'm no longer exact at math?" or "I'm no longer a numbers character?" These Declaratives are prime illustrations of a rigid mindset. the maximum of us grew up wondering this way. In school, if we spoke back something effectively and were told we're "smart", we began to trust that we would have been only smart if we had the proper solution all the time. If we can't do something perfectly, however, we have to not be clever in that vicinity.

Conversely, if we have an increased attitude, we're open to new opportunities. We accept as true that we can examine a new ability. We know that the only issue is in our very own mind.

whilst the benefits of an increased mind-set are easy to discover, it can be hard to put in force in all areas of our lifestyles. A few regions take greater work than others, and for plenty of human beings, that region of increase needs to occur in the private price range.

growth mindset on the subject of budgeting.

fixed: "I don't understand a way to govern a rate variety."

boom: "getting to know how to control a fee range will give me more freedom."

Which one would you rather become aware of? try creating a listing of your fixed mindsets and transforming them!

3. Set goals with your accomplice, so you're each on the same page

Budgeting isn't something you need to do by myself, especially if you're in a critical courting. communicate with your partner and create money desires together. This could hold you on the equal web page while making easy selections, like how many tons to spend on your niece's birthday present, or what sort of gym membership to purchase. It can additionally help keep away from frustration while you're planning for larger purchases, like how an awful lot to spend on your next romantic getaway, and financial savings plans, including retirement or your toddler's university training.

whilst you paint collectively as a pair to acquire not unusual goals, budgeting turns into less daunting. layout a budget that works for each of you, and honor that commitment via sticking to it.

4. Don't think about finances as restricting, however as freeing!

Budgeting doesn't need to be viewed in a terrible light. In reality, the great component of approximately setting a finances is that you get to determine how a good deal you get to spend on the entirety!

Don't you need to give up your shopping dependency? comprise a monthly garb allowance into your price range. involved you did not have sufficient money to pay for get-togethers or birthdays? include a financial savings line for all the parties you'll be attending that 12 months. as long as you're making extra money than you're spending, you may make your budget be just right for you.

When you're aware about where all your budgets are going, you will begin to feel a newfound feeling of freedom. not anything is in the dark. You've determined where you need to spend, store, and cut. handling your budget can be empowering in case you allow it.

5. Don't start with the end in mind.

Budgeting is a tool designed that will help you live your first-class existence. if you start with a cease goal in thoughts, it could feel extraordinarily daunting. (Who desires to focus on paying off $100k in student loans?)

alternatively, pay attention to your finances in digestible ranges. tune your progress weekly, and have fun all of the tiny wins. Did you persist with your budget in week one? awesome! Week 4? Congratulations! Soon, your finances will become a herbal part of your daily habit.

When you've gotten the grasp of it, experience unfastened to modify your budget on every occasion is important. Your profits will fluctuate, and your financial savings dreams will change through the years. Just recall, your finances need to never make you feel disadvantaged or crushed. That is not its cause.

6. Change your beliefs about budgeting.

It's as much as you to decide how you need to sense budgeting. In case you think it's going to be hard, it probably could be. in case you suppose it's going to aid you in getting the entirety you need out of lifestyles, it's going to do this for you as well.

How do you change your beliefs about budgeting? First, revisit your tale (returned to step one) and recognize why you experience a certain way approximately with money. In which did you inherit those ideals? Are you open to converting them?

Once you've determined you're open to making a trade for your mind-set, write down how you need to sense budgeting as a substitute. begin to surround yourself with individuals who percentage not unusual goals. join a fb organization that focuses on budgeting. talk to your partner about your not unusual dreams for destiny. hold an open communication about cash and be aware if you start to experience any otherwise. Slowly, your previous concepts will fade, and you may have new money beliefs to look ahead to.

In case you actually need to change your attitude around budgeting, start with this kind of region and pay attention to it for one week. As you develop, select some other place to paint. quickly, you could even find budgeting to be something you look ahead to! consider, you get to determine what your budget looks like.

The Simple Guide To Budgeting

Chapter 3: Balance is Key

Understanding Financial Balance

Economic balance is a complicated concept, but know-how it could be vital for each person and group. It refers to a country of financial balance and protection, in which an entity's earnings are sufficient to cover its charges and debts, leaving room for saving and funding.
right here are a few key factors of economic stability:

For individuals:

Cash flow management: This entails tracking your profits and fees to ensure you're spending much less than you earn. Budgeting and growing a spending plan allow you to stay inside your manner and keep away from accumulating debt.

Debt management: Having debt can affect your economic balance, as you need to devote a part of your earnings to repayments. goal to hold your debt-to-income ratio at a wholesome level and prioritize paying off high-interest debt.

Financial savings and investments: building a financial cushion through saving and investing is crucial for coping with surprising charges or emergencies. This additionally lets in you to gain long-term monetary goals, like retirement.

Economic literacy: expertise monetary standards like budgeting, debt control, and investing empowers you to make informed selections and manage your budget efficiently.

For businesses:e

Liquidity: corporations want sufficient cash on hand to fulfill their quick-time period duties. keeping adequate liquidity ensures they are able to operate easily and keep away from financial misery.

Solvency: This refers to an agency's capacity to meet its lengthy-time period debt responsibilities. A healthful stability sheet with sufficient assets to cover liabilities suggests solvency.

Profitability: generating earnings ensures enough earnings to cover expenses, reinvest inside the enterprise, and praise traders.

Economic plans making: corporations want to forecast their future monetary wishes and increase strategies to make sure they've the assets to gain their goals.

Factors Affecting Financial Balance:

Several factors can influence financial balance, including:
1. Income: The amount of money earned through employment, investments, or other sources.
2. Expenses: The cost of living, including housing, food, transportation, and other necessities.
3. Debt: The amount owed on loans, credit cards, and other liabilities.
4. Investments: The value of assets held for future growth, such as stocks, bonds, and real estate.
5. Economic conditions: Factors like inflation, interest rates, and economic growth can impact income and expenses.

Maintaining Financial Balance:

There are several ways to maintain financial balance:
1. Set financial goals: Define your short-term and long-term financial goals to guide your financial decisions.

2. Develop a budget: Track your income and expenses to understand your spending patterns and identify areas for improvement.

3. Pay off debt: prioritize paying off high-interest debt to reduce your financial burden.

4. Save and invest: Allocate a portion of your income towards savings and investments to achieve your financial goals.

5. Educate yourself: Continuously learn about financial concepts and strategies to make informed decisions.

Income vs. Expenses

At the middle of economic equilibrium lies the delicate dance among income and expenses—a dynamic interplay that determines the fitness of your monetary landscape. Getting to know the art of balancing earnings and expenses is a fundamental step towards financial well-being. let's delve into the intricacies of this vital element and explore strategies to make sure a harmonious courting between what you earn and what you spend

- **knowledge Your earnings sources**

The muse of monetary balance starts with a complete know-how of your profits resources. This includes your number one income, secondary assets such as freelance work or investments, and any passive profits streams. By having a clean assessment of your income, you can make knowledgeable selections about budgeting and monetary making plans.

- **Developing a realistic finances**

A nicely-crafted budget serves as your roadmap to financial stability. It entails categorizing your earnings and allocating price range to numerous charges, ensuring that your spending aligns along with your economic goals. through creating finances, you benefit visibility into which your cash goes and might become aware of regions for optimization or discount.

- **Prioritizing critical prices**

inside the realm of earnings vs. charges, distinguishing among wants and needs is pivotal. important costs, along with housing, utilities, and groceries, take precedence. Prioritizing these desires guarantees that your fundamental requirements are met before allocating finances to discretionary spending.

- **Curbing needless Spending**

The appeal of discretionary spending can every so often tip the balance unfavorably. Recognizing and curbing pointless expenses is a vital ability. We will discover realistic techniques for cutting lower back on non-critical spending without sacrificing your satisfaction of lifestyles, permitting you to redirect funds in the direction of savings and lengthy-term desires.

- **Adjusting Your lifestyle on your income**

Monetary stability calls for aligning your lifestyle along with your profits stage. This does not always suggest austerity; alternatively, it includes conscious picks that reflect your monetary priorities. We'll discuss strategies for adapting your life-style to make sure it is sustainable within the confines of your contemporary and future earnings.

Short-Term vs. Long-Term Financial Goals

In the voyage of personal finance, charting a direction for success includes the intentional pursuit of both brief-term objectives and lengthy-term aspirations. expertise the differences and intricacies of those goals is crucial for creating a financial strategy that aligns along with your imaginative and prescient for the destiny. be a part of us as we explore the seas of brief-time period and lengthy-time period economic goals, uncovering the strategies to navigate each leg of your economic adventure.

1. Defining brief-time period financial desires
A brief-time period monetary dreams are the waypoints along your financial adventure that typically span one year or less. These dreams often contain instantaneous needs and dreams, consisting of creating an emergency fund, paying off credit card debt, or saving for a holiday. The focus right here is on tangible, attainable goals that contribute for your monetary properly-being within the close to destiny.

2. strategies for attaining quick-time period success
meeting short-time period financial desires calls for a targeted and disciplined technique. We are able to discuss sensible techniques for budgeting, price prioritization, and leveraging extra earnings streams to expedite your development. through attaining fulfillment in the brief term, you now not simplest construct economic self assurance however additionally create a basis for tackling greater formidable long-time period goals.

3. Envisioning long-term financial success
lengthy-time period financial goals enlarge past the horizon, regularly masking periods of five years or extra. Examples encompass saving for a home, investing a child's education, or constructing a strong retirement nest egg. These objectives require a strategic and sustained attempt, emphasizing the importance of investment, wealth accumulation, and prudent monetary making plans.

4. investment strategies for lengthy-time period growth

making an investment performs a pivotal role within the pursuit of long-time period economic fulfillment. We can explore various investment vehicles, risk management strategies, and the power of compound hobby. know-how the way to combine investments into your long-time period plan empowers you to harness the capability for increase and wealth accumulation over the years.

5. Balancing quick-term Gratification with long-term planning

The key to a successful economic journey lies in placing a harmonious stability among brief-time period gratification and lengthy-term making plans. We are able to discuss how to allocate sources correctly, ensuring that on the spot desires are met whilst development in the direction of enduring financial desires stays steadfast.

The Role of Emergency Funds

inside the unpredictable seas of personal finance, unexpected challenges can arise at any second, threatening to disrupt the clean cruising of your economic ship. An emergency fund serves as your anchor, presenting balance and protection when confronted with unexpected waves. permit's delve into the important role of emergency finances and the way they contribute to your economic resilience.

1. economic balance in uncertain Waters

An emergency fund acts as an economic protection net, supplying balance in times of uncertainty. Whether or not dealing with an unexpected scientific price, unexpected car maintenance, or a transient lack of profits, having a designated fund lets in you to navigate these challenges without capsizing your usual financial balance.

2. fast reaction to Unplanned prices

existence's surprises regularly come unannounced, and the capacity to respond unexpectedly could make all the distinction. Your emergency fund is your first line of defense, providing immediate access to the budget when surprising fees rise up. This agility allows you to cope with emergencies without resorting to high-interest debt or derailing your long-time period monetary desires.

3. Peace of mind in Turbulent instances

past the economic aspects, an emergency fund contributes to peace of mind. understanding that you have an economic buffer in an area instills self belief and reduces strain, allowing you to consciousness on overcoming challenges as opposed to stressful approximate economic repercussions.

4. protection towards earnings Volatility

For people with variable profits or entrepreneurial ventures, the steadiness supplied via an emergency fund is even extra mentioned. It acts as a guard against income volatility, making sure that you may cowl critical prices at some point of lean durations without compromising your monetary fitness.

5. retaining lengthy-term financial goals

At the same time as quick-term in nature, the function of an emergency fund is interconnected along with your lengthy-term monetary goals. by weathering unexpected monetary storms with your emergency fund, you defend your capacity to live in direction toward attaining broader objectives inclusive of homeownership, training investment, or retirement financial savings.

Within the monetary narrative of your life, an emergency fund is the unsung hero—a silent mum or dad prepared to protect you from the unexpected. As we navigate the concept of economic balance in "An easy manual to Budgeting," knowledge and prioritizing the position of emergency funds guarantees that your monetary delivery remains resilient, able to cruise via both calm seas and unexpected tempests.

Importance of Emergency Funds

Inside the problematic tapestry of personal finance, the importance of an emergency fund can not be overstated. Often likened to an economic citadel, this fund stands as a pillar of resilience, offering protection against the unforeseen demanding situations that life may also hurl your way. permit's discover why an emergency fund is a cornerstone of monetary nicely-being.

- **Shielding in opposition to the sudden**

life's journey is dotted with sudden twists and turns, and economic surprises aren't any exception. Whether it is a surprising scientific expense, vehicle maintenance, or unexpected home upkeep, the true price of an emergency fund lies in its potential to behave as a defense, imparting a sturdy protection in opposition to unplanned monetary setbacks.

- **Instant reaction to economic Emergencies**

The swiftness with which economic emergencies call for interest frequently leaves little room for prolonged economic making plans. An emergency fund is designed to facilitate an instantaneous response. Having no trouble with accessible price range manners you can navigate via crises without resorting to excessive-hobby loans or disrupting your long-term monetary strategy.

- **Reducing financial pressure and anxiety**

Financial strain can take a toll on general nice-being. An emergency fund serves as a buffer, reducing tension by offering a monetary safety internet. knowing that you have a cushion to fall back on in times of crisis brings a sense of safety, allowing you to stand challenges with clearer thoughts and a steadier remedy.

- **Keeping financial Independence**

counting on external sources for monetary guidance for the duration of emergencies can compromise your independence. An emergency fund preserves your autonomy by allowing you to deal with unforeseen charges without depending on loans or help from others. This financial self-sufficiency fosters an experience of manipulation over your economic destiny.

- **Mitigating income Volatility**

For people with variable income or fee-based profits, the importance of an emergency fund is heightened. It acts as a stabilizer, mitigating the impact of earnings volatility. This guarantees that important fees are blanketed for the duration of lean periods, preventing monetary setbacks that would restrict progress in the direction of lengthy-time economic desires.

- **Safeguarding long-time period monetary desires**

whilst mostly designed for quick-term needs, an emergency fund performs a vital function in safeguarding your long-term economic aspirations. With the aid of weathering sudden financial storms without derailing your broader economic plan, this fund will become an invaluable best friend in the pursuit of desires including homeownership, schooling funding, or retirement savings.

How to Build and Maintain an Emergency Fund

An emergency fund is the financial cushion that stands between you and unexpected challenges. Building and maintaining this safety net requires a strategic approach and discipline. Let's explore actionable steps to construct and sustain an emergency fund, providing you with financial resilience in the face of life's uncertainties.

1. Establish Clear Goals:

Define the cause of your emergency fundIs it for job loss, medical emergencies, or unforeseen expenses? Having clarity on the fund's purpose guides your savings strategy.

2. Determine the Ideal Amount:

Attempt to store 3 to 6 months' worth of living expenses. Calculate essential costs like rent, utilities, groceries, and insurance to determine this baseline.

3. Start Small, but Start Today:

Initiate the process by setting achievable monthly savings goals. Even a modest amount contributes to the fund over time. The key is consistency.

4. Automate Savings:

Set up an automatic transfer to your emergency fund each month. Treating it as a non-negotiable expense ensures regular contributions without relying on willpower alone.

5. Allocate Windfalls:

Direct unexpected windfalls, such as tax refunds or work bonuses, toward your emergency fund. These infusions can significantly boost your savings.

6. Cut Unnecessary Expenses:
Analyze your spending habits and identify areas where you can cut back without sacrificing essential needs. Redirect the savings toward your emergency fund.

7. Build Gradually:
Rome wasn't built in a day, and neither is a robust emergency fund. Be patient and celebrate incremental progress. Each dollar saved is a step stones toward financial security.

8. Prioritize High-Interest Debt:
While building your emergency fund, prioritize high-interest debt payments. Once your fund reaches a comfortable level, you can allocate more towards debt repayment.

9. Separate Your Emergency Fund:
Keep your emergency fund separate from your regular checking account. Consider a dedicated savings account to prevent easy access for non-emergencies.

10. Reassess and Adjust:
Periodically reassess your living expenses and adjust your emergency fund goals accordingly. Life circumstances change, and your fund should adapt to these shifts.

11. Resist Temptation:
Discipline is crucial. Avoid dipping into your emergency fund for non-emergencies. Treat it as a financial lifeline reserved exclusively for unforeseen circumstances.

12. Regularly Review and Replenish:
Regularly review your fund's status. If you use it for a legitimate emergency, make it a priority to replenish the withdrawn amount promptly.

Building and maintaining an emergency fund is a journey marked by consistency and determination. By following these steps and staying committed to your financial goals, you'll forge a robust safety net that empowers you to navigate life's uncertainties with confidence and resilience.

Balancing Spending and Saving

Balancing spending and saving is a constant juggle, but it's essential for achieving your financial goals and building a secure future. Here are some strategies to help you find harmony between enjoying life today and preparing for tomorrow:

- **Create a Budget:**

track your income and charges for a month to apprehend your spending patterns.
Categorize your expenses: essentials (housing, food, utilities), non-essentials (entertainment, dining out, hobbies).
Allocate your income: prioritize essential expenses, allocate a percentage for saving goals, and set a limit for non-essential spending.

- **Prioritize Saving:**

Pay yourself first: Automate transfers to your savings account as soon as you receive your income.
Start small and increase gradually: Aim for 10-15% of your income initially, and incrementally increase as your financial situation improves.

- **Embrace the 50/30/20 Rule:**

Allocate 50% of your income to essential needs (housing, food, utilities).
Dedicate 30% to discretionary spending (entertainment, dining out, hobbies).
Commit 20% to savings and debt repayment.

- **Track Your Spending:**

Use budgeting apps, spreadsheets, or a simple notebook to monitor your spending daily or weekly.

Review your spending regularly and identify areas where you can cut back. Be honest and accountable: Acknowledge any overspending and adjust your plan accordingly.

- **Apply the "Needs vs. Wants" Rule:**

Before creating a buy, ask yourself if it is a "need" or a "want."
Prioritize needs like groceries and rent over wants like designer clothing or lavish vacations.
Consider cheaper alternatives or delaying purchases to fulfill your wants without compromising your savings goals.

- **Practice Mindfulness:**

Be mindful of your spending habits and triggers.
Avoid emotional spending: don't make impulsive purchases to feel better.
Look for free or low-cost alternatives to enjoy leisure activities.

- **Set Financial Goals:**

Define your short-term and long-term financial goals.
Visualize the benefits of achieving these goals: a comfortable retirement, a dream vacation, a down payment on a house.
Let your goals motivate you to stay disciplined with your spending and saving habits.

- **Make Saving Enjoyable:**

Set up automatic transfers to "treat yourself" savings goals for vacations or new experiences.
Utilize reward programs and loyalty points to boost your savings.
Celebrate milestones: acknowledge your progress and reward yourself for reaching savings targets.

- **Seek Support:**

Discuss your financial goals and challenges with a trusted friend, family member, or financial advisor.
Join online communities or support groups for motivation and accountability.

- **Review and Adapt:**

Regularly assess your budget and spending habits.
Adjust your plan as needed: life changes, unexpected expenses, or income fluctuations may require adjustments.
Balancing spending and saving is a continuous process, but by adopting these strategies and maintaining a consistent approach, you can achieve financial harmony and create a brighter future for yourself.
keep in mind, financial proper-being is an adventure, no longer a vacation spot. Celebrate your progress, learn from setbacks, and adjust your approach as needed. Enjoy life today while also investing in a secure tomorrow.

Prioritizing Needs vs. Wants

In the intricate dance of financial decision-making, the art of prioritizing needs versus wants is a strategic maneuver that shapes the trajectory of your financial well-being. This nuanced process involves discernment and intentionality as you navigate the landscape of essential requirements and discretionary desires. Let's explore the tactics for making discerning choices without echoing previously used terms.

1. Critical vs. Discretionary:
   Distinguish between critical necessities and discretionary indulgences. Prioritize expenditures that fulfill vital needs before allocating resources to optional, non-essential items.

2. Essential Expenditures:
   Identify and address indispensable expenses that sustain your basic standard of living. This includes fundamental needs such as housing, utilities, groceries, and healthcare.

3. Core Financial Obligations:
   Recognize core financial obligations that are non-negotiable for your well-being and stability. These could encompass debt repayments, insurance premiums, and essential services.

4. Non-Essential Luxuries:
   Deliberate on non-essential luxuries and evaluate their significance in your life. Consider whether these discretionary expenses align with your broader financial goals and values.

5. Strategic Allocation:
   Strategically allocate resources by focusing on fulfilling needs first before indulging in wants. This approach ensures that your financial foundation remains robust and resilient.

6. Long-Term vs. Short-Term Impact:

Assess the impact of your expenditures over both short-term and long-term horizons. Prioritize needs that contribute to long-term financial stability over fleeting wants.

7. Necessities as Foundations:

Acknowledge necessities as the foundations upon which your financial well-being rests. By securing these essentials, you create a stable platform for addressing discretionary desires.

8. Emotional vs. Rational Spending:

Evaluate spending through both emotional and rational lenses. While desires may appeal to emotions, rational analysis ensures that essential needs receive precedence.

9. Immediate Requirements:

Attend to immediate requirements before diverting resources to optional wants. This sequential approach allows you to address pressing needs without compromising financial stability.

10. Periodic Financial Audits:

Conduct periodic financial audits to reassess your spending patterns. This proactive measure enables you to refine your prioritization strategy in alignment with evolving financial goals.

11. Adaptability in Prioritization:

Embrace adaptability in your prioritization strategy. Recognize that financial priorities may shift, necessitating adjustments to accommodate changing circumstances and aspirations.

Prioritizing needs versus wants is an ongoing strategic process that requires a blend of foresight, mindfulness, and adaptability. By weaving these tactics into your financial decision-making, you orchestrate a harmonious symphony that resonates with financial stability and purpose.

Tips for Creating a Balanced Budget

1. Holistic Budgeting technique:

Adopt a complete budgeting strategy that considers all factors of your monetary life. encompass constant charges, discretionary spending, savings, and debt repayment for your budget to ensure a holistic and balanced method.

2. Prioritize excessive-hobby Debt:

Start by addressing excessive-hobby debt as a priority. Allocating a budget to lessen extremely good money owed not most effectively frees up economic assets however also contributes to standard stability for your economic portfolio.

3. Emergency Fund as a basis:

Establish and preserve an emergency fund because it is the cornerstone of your economic stability. This fund acts as a buffer, presenting a safety net at some stage in unforeseen instances and contributing to the overall balance of your financial plan.

4. Allocate for short-term and long-term goals:

Strive for stability via allocating price range for each brief-time period and long-time period economic goals. Whether or not it is saving for a holiday, buying a home, or making plans for retirement, a balanced method guarantees that your economic aspirations are addressed at every degree.

5. regular economic test-ins:

Schedule normal economics, take a look at-ins to evaluate your development and make vital adjustments. This proactive technique allows you to pick out imbalances early on and fine-track your monetary plan to align with converting situations.

6. conscious Spending and smart Saving:

Domesticate a conscious approach to spending with the aid of comparing the necessity and fee of each expense. simultaneously, enforce clever saving strategies including computerized transfers and goal-orientated saving to strike a stability among meeting immediate needs and making ready for the destiny.

developing monetary balance is an ongoing technique that calls for a blend of strategic planning, subject, and adaptableness. by incorporating those recommendations into your economic habitual, you pave the manner for a well-balanced and resilient monetary future.

The Simple Guide To Budgeting

Chapter 4: Budgeting Checklist

Creating a Personal Budget

1. Income Assessment:

Start by carefully evaluating your sources of revenue. Compile a comprehensive list of all your revenue streams, including your primary job, side gigs, freelance work, or any passive income. Understanding your income is the foundational step in creating an effective budget.

2. Identifying Fixed and Variable Expenses:

Divide your spending into classes: fixed and variable. Fixed expenses include non-negotiable costs like rent or mortgage payments, utilities, and insurance. Variable costs include spending on things like eating out, entertainment, and shopping. This distinction lays the groundwork for a more detailed and manageable budget.

3. Expense Tracking and Categorization:

Implement a system to track your expenses diligently. Utilize budgeting apps or spreadsheets to record every expenditure, no matter how small. Categorize these expenses to gain insights into your spending patterns, making it easier to identify areas for adjustment.

4. Establishing Realistic Budget Goals:

Set realistic financial goals that align with your priorities. Whether you're aiming to pay off debt, save for a vacation, or build an emergency fund, having clear and achievable objectives provides direction to your budgeting efforts. Break down these goals into manageable, monthly targets to track progress effectively.

5. Adjusting the Budget as Needed:

Recognize that life is dynamic, and your budget should be flexible to accommodate changes. Regularly review and adjust your budget based on shifts in income, expenses, or financial goals. Being adaptable ensures that your budget remains a relevant and effective tool for managing your finances.

Creating a personal budget is a dynamic process that requires attention to detail and a commitment to financial transparency. By following these steps, you lay the groundwork for a budget that not only reflects your current financial reality but also serves as a guiding tool to help you achieve your short-term and long-term financial aspirations.

Tracking and Categorizing Expenses

Tracking and categorizing expenses is an important part of financial management, whether or not for personal or commercial enterprise functions. It facilitates you to reveal your coin float, plan your budget, optimize your tax deductions, and avoid overspending. but, it may additionally be a tedious and time-consuming mission, mainly when you have multiple resources of profits and charges

- **Identify areas of overspending:** By seeing your spending habits visually, you can easily identify areas where you may be overspending and make adjustments accordingly.

- **Prioritize your spending:** Categorizing your expenses helps you allocate your resources efficiently, ensuring essential needs are met before focusing on non-essential wants.

- **Set financial goals:** Understanding your spending patterns helps you set realistic and achievable financial goals, whether it's saving for a vacation, a down payment on a house, or retirement.

- **Make informed financial decisions:** With a clear picture of your income and expenses, you can make informed financial decisions that align with your long-term goals.

Here are some effective methods for tracking and categorizing your expenses:

1. Traditional Methods:

Physical notebooks: Keep a dedicated notebook to record all your income and expenses, categorized by type (e.g., groceries, rent, entertainment).

Spreadsheets: Create a spreadsheet with columns for date, description, category, amount, and payment method. This allows for easy sorting and filtering of your data.

Monthly expense reports: Gather all your receipts and bills for the month and categorize them in a report. This method requires more time but can offer a detailed overview of your spending.

2. Digital Tools:

Budgeting apps: Utilize budgeting apps like Mint, Personal Capital, or YNAB to automatically track your spending, categorize expenses, and create budgets.

Banking apps: Many banks offer built-in budgeting tools that categorize your transactions automatically based on their merchant category codes.

Receipt scanning apps: Use apps like Expensify or Receipt Hog to scan receipts and automatically categorize your purchases.

3. Categorization Tips:

Use a consistent system: Choose a method that works best for you and stick to it for consistency.

Create relevant categories: Adapt your categories to your specific spending habits and financial goals.

Regularly review and update: Periodically review your categories and adjust them as your needs evolve.

Set spending limits: Allocate specific amounts to each category to ensure you stay within your budget.

Additional Tips:

Set up automatic transfers: Automate transfers to savings accounts and investment accounts to ensure you are consistently saving towards your goals.

Track your net worth: Monitor your net worth by tracking the value of your assets and liabilities to gauge your overall financial progress.

Seek professional guidance: Consult a financial advisor for personalized advice and strategies tailored to your financial situation.

By monitoring and categorizing your expenses, you benefit from valuable insights into your monetary habits, enabling you to make informed decisions, optimize your spending, and obtain your financial dreams with more readability and manipulation.

Common Budgeting Mistakes to Avoid

Creating and adhering to a budget is a fundamental aspect of financial success, but pitfalls abound. Recognizing and avoiding common budgeting mistakes is key to maintaining a healthy financial outlook. Here are some pitfalls to sidestep:

- **Ignoring Irregular Expenses:**
  Failing to account for irregular or periodic expenses can derail your budget. Be proactive in identifying and budgeting for annual fees, holidays, or other irregular costs to avoid financial surprises.

- **Overlooking Small Purchases:**
  Neglecting to track small, everyday expenses can add up quickly. Those coffee shop visits or impulse purchases may seem inconsequential, but collectively, they can significantly impact your budget. Account for all expenditures, no matter how minor.

- **Setting Unrealistic Goals:**
  Ambitious financial goals are commendable, but setting unrealistic targets can lead to frustration and eventual abandonment of the budget. Establish achievable milestones that align with your income and lifestyle to ensure ongoing success.

- **Neglecting Emergency Savings:**
  Failing to prioritize emergency savings is a common oversight. Unexpected expenses are inevitable, and without a financial safety net, you may find yourself resorting to high-interest debt to cover unforeseen costs. Make building and keeping an emergency fund a pinnacle precedence.

- **Not Reviewing and Adjusting:**
  A budget isn't always a static file. circumstances exchange, and your budget should evolve for this reason. Regularly review your financial plan,

adjust categories as needed, and ensure that your budget aligns with your current priorities and goals.

- **Being Too Restrictive:**
A budget is a tool for financial empowerment, not deprivation. Being overly restrictive can lead to frustration and may increase the likelihood of abandoning the budget altogether. Allow for reasonable discretionary spending to maintain a healthy balance.

- **Relying Solely on Memory:**
 Depending on memory to recall expenses is unreliable. Implement a tracking system, whether through budgeting apps, spreadsheets, or dedicated notebooks, to record and categorize expenses consistently. This ensures accuracy and facilitates informed financial decisions.

- **Neglecting Future Planning:**
Focusing solely on immediate financial concerns without planning for the future is a mistake. Allocate funds for long-term goals such as retirement, homeownership, or education to secure your financial future while maintaining a balanced budget in the present.

- **Ignoring Debt Repayment:**
 Neglecting to address high-interest debt hinders your financial progress. Prioritize debt repayment within your budget to reduce interest payments and free up more funds for savings and discretionary spending.

- **Forgetting to Communicate:**
 If you share financial responsibilities with a partner or family members, communication is vital. A lack of communication about budgetary goals, priorities, and spending habits can lead to misunderstandings and hinder the effectiveness of the budget.

By steering clear of these common budgeting mistakes, you position yourself for financial success. A well-crafted budget, coupled with mindfulness and adaptability, serves as a powerful tool in achieving your financial aspirations.

Establishing Realistic Budget Goals

developing a practical budget is one of the most vital abilities you can discover ways to manipulate your money and reap your economic goals. A finance is a plan that indicates how good a deal of profits you have, how an awful lot you spend, and how much you keep or make investments. A realistic price range is one that displays your actual earnings and fees, and allows you to balance your needs and wants. In this text, we will speak a number of the best methods to create a sensible finances, which includes:

- **Music your earnings and expenses**

Step one to growing a practical finances is to song your profits and fees for at least a month. You can use a spreadsheet, an app, or a notebook to document how much money you earn and what kind of money you spend on diverse categories, which includes housing, food, transportation, amusement, and so on. This can assist you see where your cash is going and identify your fixed and variable costs. Constant fees are those that live the same every month, consisting of hire, loan, or coverage. Variable charges are those that alternate depending on your usage or conduct, together with groceries, utilities, or dining out.

- **Set your financial goals**

The second step to growing practical finances is to set your monetary dreams, both quick-term and long-term. short-term dreams are the ones that you want to reap within a 12 months, together with saving for a vacation, paying off a credit card debt, or buying new equipment. long-term goals are those which you need to gain in greater than a yr, which include saving for retirement, buying a residence, or starting a business. Your monetary goals have to be smart: particular, measurable, viable, relevant, and time-certain. For example, in place of pronouncing "I want to store more money", you could say "I need to store $10,000 for a down charge on a residence in years".

- **Create a spending plan**

The third step to growing a sensible budget is to create a spending plan that allocates your earnings in your charges and your financial savings or investments. A famous approach to create a spending plan is the 50/30/20 rule, which shows that you spend 50% of your income for your needs, 30% for your desires, and 20% for your financial savings or investments. however, you could adjust these percentages consistent with your personal state of affairs and preferences. The key is to make certain that your spending plan covers your constant and variable expenses, as well as your financial goals.

- **Reveal and regulate your finances**

The fourth step to growing a realistic finances is to monitor and alter your price range frequently. You ought to overview your finances as a minimum once a month to look in case you are sticking to your spending plan and meeting your financial desires. You need to also compare your real income and expenses in your anticipated ones, and become aware of any gaps or discrepancies. if you locate which you are spending greater than you earn, or which you are not saving enough on your desires, you need to alter your price range as a result. You can try this by increasing your income, reducing your costs, or prioritizing your dreams.

- **Use tools and resources**

The fifth step to developing a practical finances is to use equipment and assets that let you along with your budgeting manner. There are numerous apps, web sites, books, and podcasts that can offer you guidelines, advice, and guidance on how to create and hold a sensible budget. Some examples are Mint, You want finances, the whole money Makeover, and The Dave Ramsey display. you can additionally seek professional assistance from a financial planner, a counselor, or a coach if you need greater personalized or specialized help.

- **Celebrate your progress**

The sixth and very last step to growing a realistic budget is to rejoice in your development and praise yourself in your achievements. Budgeting may be tough and worrying, however it can also be profitable and pleasant. You need to acknowledge your efforts and successes, and deal with yourself to something that makes you glad and prompted. for instance, you could purchase yourself a brand new e-book, watch a film, or have a pleasing meal. however, make certain that your rewards are inside your budget and do not derail your monetary dreams. recall, developing a realistic finances isn't a one-time event, but a continuous manner that calls for subject, dedication, and versatility.

Setting Short-Term and Long-Term Financial Objectives

Establishing a roadmap in your financial adventure involves setting each brief-term and lengthy-term goals. These goals, when aligned along with your aspirations, create a comprehensive plan for economic fulfillment. here is a manual to help you chart your direction:

Setting short-term financial goals:

1. Emergency Fund:
 Prioritize constructing an emergency fund as a short-term goal. intention to save 3 to 6 months' worth of living costs to offer a monetary protection internet for sudden challenges.

2. Debt reimbursement:
 Set a goal for reducing excessive-interest debt. Allocate a selected amount every month to pay down credit card balances or other amazing loans. This short-time period objective improves your economic fitness and frees up resources for other desires.

3. monthly savings targets:
 Set up month-to-month savings targets for precise functions, including a vacation fund, home development projects, or a brand new gadget. These brief-time period financial savings goals provide a sense of achievement and help you control discretionary spending.

4. training and ability development:
 Keep in mind quick-term targets associated with training and talent development. This will contain budgeting for a route, workshop, or certification program that complements your expert talents and potentially will increase your income.

5. fitness and well being:

Encompass quick-term desires related to fitness and well being. Allocate finances for fitness center memberships, wellbeing packages, or different activities that contribute for your bodily and intellectual property-being.

Setting long-term financial goals:

1. Retirement savings:

Prioritize long-time period targets which include retirement financial savings. decide how a good deal you need to retire comfortably and set annual financial savings goals. Starting early maximizes the power of compounding.

2. Homeownership:

If homeownership is a goal, define the steps needed to store for a down charge. This lengthy-time period objective may additionally contain building an additional savings fund and handling your credit score to qualify for a mortgage.

3. funding Portfolio boom:

expand an extended-time period strategy for developing your funding portfolio. Set objectives for diversification, threat tolerance, and preferred returns. regularly assess and modify your investment plan based totally on converting marketplace situations.

4. training funding:

Plan for training investment if you have youngsters or count on academic expenses. establish savings dreams for college finances or other educational needs, deliberating inflation and the rising expenses of training.

5. profession development and income boom:

Define long-term goals associated with career advancement and profits boom. This can involve obtaining superior degrees, gaining certifications, or strategically positioning yourself for promotions or career adjustments.

6. Legacy planning:

Include objectives associated with legacy planning, such as property making plans and wealth transfer. This guarantees that your monetary legacy aligns together with your values and offers for future generations.

7. Philanthropy and Giving returned:

If philanthropy is critical to you, set lengthy-time period desires for charitable contributions or setting up a basis. planning for impactful giving lets you combine philanthropy into your normal monetary plan.

Life circumstances change, and your goals should adapt accordingly.

Specificity and Measurability:

Absolutely outline your objectives in particular and measurable terms. This enhances your potential to tune development and have fun achievements.

Alignment with Values:

Make certain that your economic objectives align along with your values and priorities. This alignment increases motivation and commitment to your goals.

Ordinary overview and Adjustment:

Periodically overview your monetary targets. lifestyles, occasions exchange, and your desires ought to adapt as an end result. Regular exams will let you regulate your financial objectives in response to evolving priorities.

By strategically setting each quick-time period and long-time period financial objectives, you create a dynamic and useful economic plan. This roadmap not only courses your current monetary choices however also propels you closer to a destiny of monetary security and fulfillment.

The Simple Guide To Budgeting

Adjusting the Budget as Needed

1. everyday financial take a look at-ins
- **Frequency topics:**

Schedule everyday monetary test-ins to look at your charge variety. This may be a monthly or quarterly workout.Regularity guarantees that you live proactive in handling your budget and right away address any necessary modifications.

- **profits and prices:**

In the course of these check-ins, examine modifications in your profits and expenses. Are there fluctuations in your profits? Have unexpected fees arisen? figuring out shifts to your monetary landscape allows for timely adjustments for your finances.

- **evaluate dreams:**

Examine your progress in the direction of economic dreams. If sure targets are consistently challenging to meet or if priorities have shifted, do not forget modifying your goals to align with current occasions and aspirations.

2. life events and adjustments:
- **Most important lifestyles adjustments:**

Understand that essential life adjustments necessitate finances adjustments. occasions along with a new job, marriage, childbirth, or shopping a domestic can appreciably impact your economic state of affairs. think again your price variety to house those modifications.

- **Flexibility is prime:**

Embody the power to adapt your budget as needed. A rigid finances that doesn't account for existence's twists and turns may also turn out to be impractical. whether it is a wonderful change like an income increase or a challenging event like a scientific expense, regulate your budget to reflect your contemporary truth.

- **Emergency Fund usage:**

In case you come across sudden prices, do not hesitate to utilize your emergency fund. It exists precisely for such conditions. modify your finances to fill up the fund, keeping its readiness for destiny unforeseen circumstances.

by incorporating these outlines into your economic habits, you create resilient finances which can navigate the ever-converting landscape of your financial life. Ordinary take a look at-ins and adaptability empower you to proactively manage your budget, making sure it stays a dynamic tool that reflects your contemporary wishes and goals.

The Simple Guide To Budgeting

Chapter 5: Investing for the Future

Introduction to Investing

Investing is a strong tool that can help a person get richer and reach their financial goals. Investing is a key way to reach your financial goals, whether they are to build a comfortable nest egg for retirement, pay for your child's education, or just make your general financial situation safer. We will talk about the basic ideas of trading in this introduction. We will stress how important it is to understand risk, diversification, and planning for the long run.

Without getting too technical, investing just means putting money somewhere with the hope that it will earn money back over time. This return usually comes in the form of interest, earnings, or capital growth. When you save, your money is kept in a safe and easy-to-reach account. When you invest, on the other hand, you put your money into different financial tools in the hopes that they will grow faster than regular savings accounts.

- **Purpose of Investing:**

The primary purpose of investing is to make money grow over time. Investors aim to generate returns that outpace inflation, allowing their money to maintain or increase its purchasing power.

- **Risk and Return:**

There's a direct dating among risk and capacity return. Usually, investments with better capability returns include a better threat.

Understanding risk tolerance is crucial for investors to ensure their investment choices align with their comfort level.

Diversification:

Diversification involves spreading investments across different asset classes and individual securities to reduce risk.

A diversified portfolio is less vulnerable to the poor performance of a single investment.

- **Time Horizon:**

The time horizon refers back to the length of time an investor expects to preserve funding before needing to get admission to the budget.

Longer time horizons may allow investors to take on more risk and potentially benefit from compounding returns.

- **Compounding:**

Compounding is the process where the returns on an investment generate earnings, and those earnings, in turn, generate more earnings.

Over time, compounding can significantly enhance the growth of an investment.

- **Investment Accounts:**

Investors typically use various accounts for investing, such as individual brokerage accounts, retirement accounts (e.g., 401(k) or IRA), and education savings accounts (e.g., 529 plans).

- **Market Research:**

Informed investing involves conducting research on potential investments, considering factors like financial health, market trends, and economic conditions.

Staying informed about the performance of investments is crucial for making sound decisions.

- **Long-Term Perspective:**

Successful making an investment frequently requires an extended-term perspective. Short-term market fluctuations are common, and a patient approach can help investors ride out volatility.

- **Financial goals:**

buyers have to align their investment approach with their economic desires, whether or not it is saving for retirement, shopping for a domestic, investment education, or accomplishing other milestones.

In conclusion, investing is a powerful tool for constructing wealth, but it comes with dangers. It's essential for individuals to educate themselves, apprehend their financial desires, check chance tolerance, and increase a well-various investment strategy. Looking for professional advice and staying informed about market situations can make contributions to a hit investing over the long term.

Benefits of Investing

1. Wealth Accumulation:
Investing gives a powerful road for gathering wealth through the years. With the aid of setting cash to paintings in diverse investment automobiles, people have the capability to generate returns that outpace traditional savings methods, contributing to lengthy-time period financial increase.

2. Beat Inflation:
Making an investment gives a means to fight the eroding results of inflation. Unlike stagnant coins, investments have the ability to provide returns that hold pace with or exceed the charge of inflation, keeping or even increasing shopping power through the years.

3. Diversification for risk management:
Diversifying investments through exclusive asset training—such as stocks, bonds, and real estate—allows unfolding risk. This diversification method can mitigate the impact of negative-acting investments, improving the general balance of a portfolio.

4. Profits technology:
Positive investments, along with dividend-paying stocks or bonds, can provide a constant move of income. These extra profits can complement earnings from employment and make contributions to financial protection, particularly in the course of retirement.

5. Long-time period growth capacity:
investing with an extended-term attitude allows people to harness the electricity of compounding. Through the years, earnings from investments generate additional returns, creating a snowball impact that could extensively enhance common portfolio growth.

6. Retirement planning:
Making an investment is a critical issue of effective retirement making plans. By always contributing to retirement bills and strategically investing those finances, individuals can construct a nest egg that supports a secure and financially comfortable retirement.

7. Participation in financial growth:
Making an investment lets individuals take part in the increase of businesses and economies. proudly owning stocks of agencies via stocks or making an investment in marketplace finances means that as those entities prosper, traders may proportion in their fulfillment via expanded asset values.

8. Attaining financial desires:
Whether saving for a domestic, funding schooling, or realizing a dream excursion, making an investment can be tailored to precise economic goals. The capacity for better returns in comparison to standard savings techniques hastens development in the direction of achieving those aspirations.

9. Tax efficiency:
Positive investment strategies and debts provide tax benefits. know-how and strategically making use of these possibilities can beautify common after-tax returns, optimizing the performance of the funding portfolio.

10. Empowerment through financial Literacy:
Making an investment cultivates financial literacy and empowerment. As people learn about different funding alternatives, risk control strategies, and market dynamics, they benefit from a deeper understanding in their financial landscape and might make knowledgeable decisions aligned with their dreams.

With the aid of recognizing and harnessing those advantages, people can leverage investing as a dynamic tool to cozy their financial future, reap dreams, and navigate the ever-converting panorama of private finance.

Different Investment Vehicles

1.shares:
- **possession in businesses:**

stocks constitute possession in an agency. investors buy stocks of an agency's inventory, turning into partial proprietors. inventory values can differ based totally on the enterprise's overall performance and marketplace conditions.

2. Bonds:
- **fixed-earnings Securities:**

Bonds are debt gadgets where traders lend cash to an entity, along with a government or corporation, in trade for periodic interest bills and the return of the foremost amount at maturity. Bonds are commonly considered a decrease-threat as compared to stocks.

3. Mutual funds:
- **Varied Portfolios:**

Mutual price range pools money from multiple buyers to put money into an assorted portfolio of stocks, bonds, or other securities. They offer immediate diversification, controlled by means of professional fund managers.

4. alternate-Traded price range (ETFs):
- **Marketplace-Traded Index budget:**

ETFs are much like mutual finances however change on stock exchanges like man or woman stocks. They frequently tune specific marketplace indexes, providing diversification and liquidity.

5. Real estate investment Trusts (REITs):
- **Actual estate ownership:**

REITs permit traders to personal stocks in actual estate portfolios. These trusts put money into earnings-producing actual estate properties which includes business homes, residential complexes, or infrastructure.

6. savings bills and certificates of Deposit (CDs):
- **Low-hazard, Low-go back alternatives:**

savings money owed and CDs are low-danger, low-go back options presented with the aid of banks. Even as they provide protection for principal quantities, returns are commonly lower compared to different funding cars.

7. alternatives and Derivatives:
- **Complex monetary units:**

options and derivatives are financial gadgets derived from underlying property. These can be complex and involve contracts primarily based on the destiny charge actions of assets like stocks or commodities.

8. Cryptocurrencies:
- **Digital property:**

Cryptocurrencies, such as Bitcoin and Ethereum, are digital or virtual currencies that employ encryption to secure their transactions. Those belongings operate on decentralized blockchain technology and have gained reputation as alternative investments.

9. valuable Metals:
- **Tangible property:**

Investing in treasured metals like gold and silver presents a hedge against inflation and economic uncertainties. buyers can buy physical metals or spend money on change-traded products tied to steel fees.

10. Peer-to-Peer Lending:
- **Direct Lending systems:**

Peer-to-peer lending platforms connect debtors with man or woman creditors. investors can earn a hobby by lending cash immediately to people or small corporations.

11. Collectibles and alternative Investments:
- **Tangible assets with particular price:**

Collectibles, art, and alternative investments constitute non-traditional assets. Those can include antique cars, satisfactory art, or maybe investments in rare stamps, providing particular value and ability returns.

knowledge of the traits, dangers, and capability returns related to every funding automobile empowers investors to construct diverse portfolios aligned with their economic desires and chance tolerance.

Incorporating Investments into Your Budget

1. define funding dreams:

Absolutely articulate your funding desires inside the broader context of your financial plan. whether it's saving for retirement, a domestic buy, or training, align your investments with particular goals to guide your budgetary selections.

2. check risk Tolerance:

Examine your chance tolerance earlier than incorporating investments into your budget. understand how at ease you are with market fluctuations and tailor your funding approach to align along with your threat tolerance.

3. determine funding quantity:

Allocate a selected portion of your finances to investments. This can be a percentage of your month-to-month earnings devoted to constructing a diversified funding portfolio. make sure that this amount complements your other financial commitments and obligations.

4. Emergency Fund attention:

Prioritize preserving or building an emergency fund earlier than allocating a full-size budget to investments. An emergency fund serves as an economic safety internet and gives peace of thoughts, especially in times of surprising fees.

5. price range for ordinary Contributions:

Treat your investments as an everyday rate on your budget. set up a disciplined method with the aid of allocating a fixed amount each month on your funding accounts. Consistency in contributions is key to a long-time period boom.

6. utilize computerized Transfers:

Simplify the investment process by way of putting in automated transfers out of your checking account in your investment money owed. Automating contributions ensures that you live on target together with your investment goals, minimizing the temptation to divert budget someplace else.

7. Diversify Your Portfolio:

Plan for diversification within your finances. Allocate price range across distinct investment vehicles such as shares, bonds, and other property to unfold risk and doubtlessly decorate returns. Diversification is an essential approach for handling risk.

8. evaluate and regulate Periodically:

Schedule ordinary reviews of your investment portfolio in the context of your typical budget. check your development in the direction of dreams, modify contributions as your financial situation evolves, and rebalance your portfolio to maintain diversification.

9. component in expenses and Taxes:

Do not forget transaction charges, control fees, and tax implications when budgeting for investments. Those fees can affect your standard returns, so it is crucial to account for them on your budgetary making plans.

10. teach yourself:

Make an investment of time in monetary education to make knowledgeable selections. apprehend the characteristics of various funding options, risk factors, and capability returns. information empowers you to navigate the complexities of the investment landscape.

11. Screen monetary and market trends:

Stay knowledgeable about monetary and market developments that could affect your investments. While an extended-time period method is typically really helpful, being privy to relevant trends permits you to make informed selections about your portfolio.

By seamlessly integrating investments into your budget with those considerations, you create an economic framework that not simplest supports your contemporary way of life but additionally lays the foundation for long-term wealth accumulation and monetary safety.

Determining Investment Goals

- **Clarify economic targets:**

  Start by articulating your broader financial dreams. Whether or not it's saving for retirement, buying a domestic, investment education, or attaining economic independence, understanding your overarching targets provides direction to your funding approach.

- **Establish Time Horizons:**

  Differentiate among short-term and lengthy-term goals. quick-term goals, inclusive of a down payment on a house, can also have a selected time-frame, while long-time period desires like retirement making plans involve a greater extended horizon. This distinction impacts your funding approach and threat tolerance.

- **Quantify target amounts:**

  Quantify the specific quantities required to obtain every intention. Having clear, measurable targets allows you to evaluate progress and decide the level of funding needed to reach every goal. consider elements like inflation and destiny prices while estimating target quantities.

- **Prioritize goals:**

  Prioritize your dreams based totally on their importance and urgency. At the same time as some goals, like an emergency fund, may additionally take precedence, others can be ranked based totally on your personal values and timelines. This prioritization allows you to guide your allocation of assets.

- **Keep in mind chance Tolerance:**

  assess your risk tolerance for each funding intention. distinct desires may additionally warrant exceptional threat stages. As an instance, long-time period dreams may have the funds for a better risk tolerance, allowing for probably better returns, at the same time as brief-time dreams may require a greater conservative approach to shield capital.

- **Evaluate income and costs:**

Examine your present day earnings and fees. apprehend how much discretionary profits you may allocate closer to investments after covering critical residing expenses. This assessment forms the idea for figuring out the feasibility of your funding desires within your contemporary monetary landscape.

- **Aspect in life occasions:**

Consider lifestyle events which could affect your dreams. occasions like marriage, the beginning of a toddler, or a career trade can impact your financial priorities. expecting and factoring in those existence events ensures that your funding dreams stay aligned along with your evolving occasions.

- **Alter for converting instances:**

Understand that circumstances alternate over time. Be organized to conform your funding desires in reaction to existence changes, economic conditions, or shifts in private priorities. regularly reviewing and adjusting your goals guarantees they remain applicable and possible.

- **Account for Inflation:**

Aspect within the impact of inflation for your investment dreams. modify goal quantities to account for the eroding effect of inflation through the years. This proactive step guarantees that your goals are sensible in terms of future buying electricity.

- **Seeking for professional steerage:**

Bear in mind in search of recommendation from financial specialists, specifically for complicated dreams or investment strategies. economic advisors can offer insights, assist set practical desires, and manual you in crafting a comprehensive funding plan aligned with your aspirations.

By methodically figuring out your investment desires through those steps, you create a roadmap that no longer best courses your investment selections however additionally aligns together with your broader financial vision.

Allocating Funds for Investments

Four Key Outlines for Allocating Funds to Investments

1. Define Investment Objectives:
Clarity in Goals:
Clearly define your investment objectives, specifying the purpose of each allocation. Whether it's long-term wealth accumulation, retirement planning, or funding a specific goal, understanding the purpose helps shape the strategy for allocating funds.

Categorize Objectives:
Categorize objectives based on time horizon and risk tolerance. Short-term goals, such as a down payment on a house, may warrant a more conservative allocation, while long-term goals, like retirement, may allow for a more growth-oriented approach.

2. Determine Risk Tolerance:
Risk-Return Balance:
Assess your risk tolerance to strike a balance between risk and return. Conservative investors may prefer a larger allocation to more stable assets like bonds, while those with a higher risk tolerance may allocate more to growth-oriented investments such as stocks.

Diversification Strategy:
Plan for diversification within your allocation. Diversifying across asset classes—stocks, bonds, real estate, etc.—helps spread risk. Consider the

correlation between different assets to create a well-balanced and resilient portfolio.

3. Establish Asset Allocation Strategy:
Strategic Asset Mix:
Define your asset allocation strategy by determining the percentage of funds allocated to each asset class. Common asset classes include equities, fixed income, and alternative investments. This strategic mix aligns with your risk tolerance, investment goals, and time horizon.

Rebalance Periodically:
Recognize that market fluctuations can alter your asset allocation. Periodically rebalance your portfolio to hold the preferred mix. Rebalancing involves selling or buying assets to bring the allocation back in line with your strategic plan.

4. Allocate Based on Financial Capacity:
Assess Financial Landscape:
Evaluate your current financial capacity for investment. Consider your income, expenses, and other financial obligations. The amount you allocate to investments should be sustainable within your overall budgetary framework.

Prioritize Emergency Fund:
Before allocating substantial funds to investments, ensure that you have a well-funded emergency fund. Having a financial safety net helps cover unexpected expenses and prevents the need to liquidate investments during emergencies.

Systematic Contributions:

Enforce a systematic technique to contribute budget to your investments. Whether it is a set monthly contribution or a percentage of your income, consistency is prime. Systematic contributions assist you're taking the gain of dollar-fee averaging and instill area for your investment strategy.

By following these outlines, you create a strategic approach to allocating a budget for investments that is aligned with your monetary goals, danger tolerance, and standard economic well-being. This considerate method enhances the likelihood of achieving your funding targets whilst successfully dealing with risk

Risk Management in Investing

1. understand Your risk Tolerance:
- **Self-assessment:**

start with the aid of undertaking an intensive self-evaluation to apprehend your chance tolerance. recollect elements which include your economic dreams, time horizon, and emotional resilience within the face of market fluctuations. This self-consciousness paperwork is the inspiration for powerful chance control.

- **Align Investments with danger Tolerance:**

make sure that your investment alternatives align with your recognized danger tolerance. when you have a low tolerance for volatility, consciousness on extra conservative investments. If you could withstand market fluctuations, consider a greater increase-oriented technique.

2. Diversify Your Portfolio:
- **Unfold chance throughout assets:**

enforce diversification as an essential threat control strategy. Allocate your investments across one of a kind asset lessons (shares, bonds, actual estate, etc.) and industries. Diversification facilitates mitigate the effect of bad performance in any single investment.

- **Rebalance Periodically:**

Periodically rebalance your portfolio to hold the desired level of diversification. Market fluctuations can motivate shifts in your asset allocation. Rebalancing involves adjusting your portfolio again to its authentic strategic mix, reducing publicity to over-acting assets and shopping for under-performing ones.

3. Set realistic expectations:
- **Marketplace Volatility awareness:**

acknowledge that markets can be risky, and funding values can also range. placing realistic expectancies about capability marketplace movements facilitates you to live resiliently in the course of durations of uncertainty.

- **Long-time period perspective:**

Adopt a long-term angle in relation to investments. quick-time period marketplace fluctuations are common, however a focus on the long-term growth ability of your investments can assist resist brief downturns.

4. Emergency Fund and Liquidity:
- **Hold an adequate Emergency Fund:**

Prioritize the renovation of an ok emergency fund. An emergency fund serves as a monetary safety internet, allowing you to cover surprising prices while not having to promote investments at some stage in marketplace downturns.

- **Make sure Liquidity for short-term needs:**

evaluate your liquidity desires for quick-term dreams. ensure that price ranges required for quick-time period targets are stored in greater liquid and strong investments to avoid the effect of marketplace volatility when having access to those funds.

5. Stay informed and knowledgeable:
- **Continuous financial schooling:**

stay informed about marketplace trends, economic indicators, and modifications inside the funding panorama. Non-stop financial education empowers you to make informed choices, apprehend risks, and adapt your strategy primarily based on evolving market situations.

- **Professional recommendation:**

do not forget searching for recommendation from monetary experts, particularly for complicated investment techniques or at some point of turbulent market situations. expert guidance can offer valuable insights and help you make nicely-informed decisions aligned together with your hazard tolerance and financial desires.

6. Often evaluation and adjust:
- **Periodic Portfolio evaluate:**

time table normal opinions of your investment portfolio. assess your financial goals, threat tolerance, and usual market situations. regulate your investment method as needed to align with changes in your existence situations and the monetary surroundings.

by integrating these threat management practices into your funding method, you create a resilient approach that no longer simplest seeks growth but also safeguards your financial nicely-being inside the face of market uncertainties.

The Simple Guide To Budgeting

Chapter 6: Advanced Budgeting Strategies

Debt Management

Debt control refers back to the process of organizing and controlling debt in a way that minimizes monetary threat and maximizes the ability to fulfill financial desires. It involves assessing one's debt situation, growing a plan to pay off money owed, and enforcing strategies to prevent destiny debt-related problems.

Debt management is critical for people who have taken on loans, credit score card debt, or other types of debt, in addition to businesses that rely on borrowing to finance their operations.

Debt may be a significant burden, impacting your monetary security and hindering your ability to acquire your desires. Effective debt control is vital for regaining management of your budget and paving the way for financial freedom.

here are some key techniques for effective debt management:

1. investigate Your Debt state of affairs:
- **music your debts:** Create a comprehensive list of all your debts, along with the quantity owed, hobby rates, and minimal payments.

Calculate your debt-to-income ratio: analyze the percentage of your income that goes towards debt payments. ideally, intention for a debt-to-earnings ratio beneath 36%.

discover excessive-interest debts: Prioritize paying off money owed with the very best hobby costs first, as these accrue the maximum vast charges over the years.

2. increase a Debt reimbursement Plan:

- **Create a budget:** music your profits and prices to discover areas in which you may cut back and loose up finances for debt repayment.

recollect exclusive debt repayment strategies: discover strategies like the snowball approach (paying off smaller money owed first) or the avalanche approach (prioritizing high-hobby debts).

Set realistic desires: destroy down your debt repayment into smaller, workable dreams to hold motivation and music development.

3. discover Debt comfort alternatives:

- **Debt consolidation:** integrate multiple debts into a unmarried mortgage with a decreased hobby fee, simplifying your reimbursement manner and doubtlessly saving money on interest prices.

- **Debt agreement:** Negotiate with creditors for a reduced debt quantity in alternate for a lump-sum fee. This could be a risky option, and it is critical to searching for professional guidance earlier than intending.

- **bankruptcy:** This must be taken into consideration as a remaining resort, as it incorporates significant monetary and criminal outcomes.

4. build an Emergency Fund:

intention to shop three-6 months well worth of dwelling charges in an emergency fund to cowl sudden costs and keep away from relying on debt for the duration of monetary emergencies.
Having an emergency fund can help you keep away from taking on extra debt and derail your debt repayment progress.

5. put in force Behavioral modifications:

Address the basis cause of your debt: pick out the reasons at the back of your debt accumulation and cope with them to save you future economic difficulties.

Expand healthy spending behavior: Create finances, music your spending, and prioritize wishes over desires to keep away from pointless debt accumulation.

Searching for assistance and accountability: proportion your debt compensation desires with relied on buddies or circle of relatives for guide and motivation. don't forget searching for professional economic counseling if wanted.

Remember debt control is an adventure, no longer a vacation spot. It calls for dedication, area, and consistent attempt. By means of implementing those techniques and seeking expert help whilst wanted, you may regain control of your budget, conquer debt, and acquire economic freedom.

Identifying and Prioritizing Debt

Effective debt management starts with a clear understanding of your financial situation. Identifying and prioritizing your debts is crucial for developing a strategic plan to overcome them and achieve financial freedom.

Here's how you can effectively identify and prioritize your debt:

1. Create a Comprehensive Debt Inventory:

- **List All Debts:**

    Start by putting together a comprehensive list of all your debts. Include credit cards, loans, mortgages, medical bills, and any other outstanding balances. This debt inventory provides a clear snapshot of your financial obligations.

- **Gather Details:**

    Note down essential details for each debt, such as the outstanding balance, interest rate, minimum monthly payment, and the creditor. Having this information at your fingertips is essential for informed decision-making.

2. Understand the Types of Debt:

- **Categorize Debts:**

    Categorize your debts into different sorts, such as:

    High-Interest Debt: Debts with high-interest rates, like credit cards, often demand immediate attention.

Secured Debt: Debts tied to collateral, such as a mortgage or car loan.

Unsecured Debt: Debts without specific collateral, like medical bills or personal loans.

- **Assess Priority:**
Evaluate the urgency and impact of each debt type on your overall financial health. Prioritize debts that can have severe consequences for non-payment or those with the highest interest rates.

3. Examine Interest Rates:
- **Identify High-Interest Debts:**
Focus on debts with high-interest rates, as they tend to accumulate more interest over time. Tackling these debts first can save you money in the long run.

- **Consider Consolidation:**
Explore the possibility of consolidating high-interest debts through methods like balance transfers or debt consolidation loans. This can streamline payments and potentially lower overall interest rates.

4. Assess Repayment Terms:
- **Short-Term vs. Long-Term Debts:**
Differentiate between short-term and long-term debts. Short-term debts, like credit card balances, may demand immediate attention, while long-term debts, such as a mortgage, require consistent but manageable payments.

- **Evaluate Repayment Terms:**
Assess the repayment terms of each debt. Some debts may have flexible repayment options, while others may come with stricter terms. Understanding these terms helps you plan your repayment strategy.

5. Consider Secured vs. Unsecured Debts:
- **Protect Collateral for Secured Debts:**
If you have secured debts tied to collateral (e.g., a mortgage or car loan), prioritize these to protect your assets. Non-payment on secured debts can lead to the loss of the associated property.

- **Negotiate with Creditors:**

For unsecured debts, like medical bills or personal loans, consider negotiating with creditors. Many creditors are inclined to paint with individuals to create achievable reimbursement plans.

6. Evaluate Impact on Credit Score:

- **Understand Credit Implications:**

Recognize the impact of each debt on your credit score. Delinquent payments can harm your creditworthiness, potentially affecting your ability to secure favorable terms for future credit.

- **Address Delinquent Accounts:**

If any accounts are already delinquent, prioritize bringing them current. Timely payments positively impact your credit score and demonstrate responsible financial behavior.

7. Develop a Repayment Plan:

- **Craft a Systematic Plan:**

Based on your assessments, craft a systematic repayment plan. This plan should outline how much you'll allocate to each debt, considering your budget constraints and financial goals.

- **Consider Snowball or Avalanche Methods:**

Explore popular repayment methods like the snowball or avalanche methods. The snowball method involves paying off debts with the smallest balances first, while the avalanche method prioritizes debts with the highest interest rates.

Tax planning

Navigating the complex waters of tax regulations is an essential aspect of managing your finances efficiently. here is a comprehensive manual to help you chart a path for strategic tax making plans:

1. understand Your Tax situation:
- **Assessment Tax documents:**

start with the aid of reviewing your beyond tax returns and know-how your contemporary tax scenario. take a look at earnings resources, deductions, and credit to discover regions for capability optimization.

- **Anticipate modifications:**

Anticipate any modifications in your economic scenario which could affect your taxes. Those changes could consist of process transitions, marriage, homeownership, or other full-size lifestyle activities.

2. Leverage Tax-Advantaged debts:
- **Make a contribution to Retirement money owed:**

Maximize contributions to tax-advantaged retirement bills which includes 401(ok)s, IRAs, or Roth IRAs. Those contributions now not handiest at ease your destiny but also provide instantaneous tax blessings.

- **Discover fitness financial savings money owed (HSAs):**

If eligible, make a contribution to an HSA for capacity triple-tax blessings—tax-deductible contributions, tax-unfastened increase, and tax-free withdrawals for qualified clinical expenses.

3. Optimize Deductions and credits:
- **Itemize or Take the standard Deduction:**

examine whether itemizing deductions or taking the standard deduction is more fantastic in your situation. factors including homeownership, charitable contributions, and sizable medical prices can have an impact on this decision.

- **Discover Tax credits:**

Discover and take advantage of available tax credits. commonplace credits consist of the child Tax credit, Earned profits Tax credit, and training-associated credits. credits immediately reduce your tax legal responsibility.

4. Plan for Capital profits and Losses:
- **Recognize Capital gains Tax charges:**

Be privy to the exclusive tax prices for quick-time period and lengthy-term capital gains. Strategically time the sale of investments to reduce capital profits taxes.

- **Offset gains with Losses:**

Offset capital gains with capital losses. When you have investments which have declined in cost, bear in mind promoting them to offset gains and decrease your typical tax liability.

5. consider Tax-green Investments:
- **Spend money on Tax-efficient finances:**

pick out tax-green investment automobiles, such as index finances or tax-controlled funds, to reduce taxable distributions. Those funds' intention to optimize after-tax returns.

- **Discover Tax-Advantaged Investments:**

Recollect investments with specific tax blessings, like municipal bonds, which generate tax-unfastened hobby income on the federal level.

6. examine enterprise structures:
- **Select the correct business shape**

If you're an enterprise owner or thinking about entrepreneurship, evaluate the tax implications of various enterprise systems. choices like sole proprietorship, LLC, S enterprise, or C organization can significantly impact your tax legal responsibility.

- **Make use of Small business Deductions:**

Leverage small commercial enterprise deductions, together with the ones for home places of work, gadget purchases, and commercial enterprise-associated charges. Proper file-maintaining is crucial to maximize those deductions.

7. Plan for property and gift Taxes:
- **Apprehend estate Tax Exemptions:**

Be aware about property tax exemptions and plan your estate as a result. proper property making plans can assist decrease the impact of estate taxes for your heirs.

- **Leverage present Exclusions:**

Take advantage of annual present exclusions to transfer assets to heirs tax-free. Strategic gifting can help reduce your taxable estate.

8. live informed approximately Tax law adjustments:
- **Keep Abreast of Tax law Updates:**

stay knowledgeable about changes in tax laws that can affect your monetary scenario. frequently take a look at for updates to tax codes and guidelines to make sure your techniques continue to be powerful.

- **Seek advice from Tax specialists:**

In case your financial situation is complex or tax laws go through big adjustments, consult tax professionals for personalized recommendations. Their knowledge will let you navigate elaborate tax situations.

9. organize and maintain facts:
- **Maintain targeted information:**

maintain thorough facts of your monetary transactions, deductions, and credits. nicely-prepared records make tax education extra efficient and help substantiate your claims inside the occasion of an audit.

10. Plan in advance for Retirement:
- **Remember Tax-green Withdrawal techniques:**

while coming near retirement, plan for tax-green withdrawal strategies from retirement accounts. A properly-concept-out method can minimize tax implications throughout your retirement years.

- **Element in Required minimum Distributions (RMDs):**
understand RMD necessities for retirement debts and plan for their impact on your tax scenario. Failure to take RMDs can result in penalties.

Strategic tax planning is a non-stop system that evolves with changes in your economic lifestyles and tax laws. through proactively handling your tax state of affairs, you optimize your financial assets and pave the way for long-term economic success.

Utilizing Tax-Advantaged Accounts

Tax-advantaged money owed provides several blessings for individuals looking to maximize their wealth and minimize their tax burden. Those payments offer specific features like tax-deferred growth, tax-loose withdrawals and contribution deductions, making them a powerful system for long-term economic planning.

Right here are some key benefits of utilizing tax-advantaged money owed:
- **Tax-Deferred increase:**

Investments in these accounts develop ooo like
without
Investments in these accounts grow without taxation: You do not pay taxes on your investment earnings until you withdraw the cash, permitting your wealth to compound quicker.

Maximize the power of compounding: This exponential increase appreciably increases your lengthy-time period wealth in comparison to taxable investments.

- **Tax-free Withdrawals:**

positive money owed offers tax-free withdrawals: This indicates you may withdraw your money in retirement without paying taxes on the income.

Retire quite simply: Tax-unfastened withdrawals can notably grow your retirement earnings and provide more economic security.

- **Contribution Deductions:**

Reduce your taxable profits: Contributions to some debts are tax-deductible, decreasing your typical tax liability for the 12 months.

Boom disposable profits: This permits you to store more money and further accelerate your wealth accumulation.

- **Diversification alternatives:**

Spend money on various asset training: Many tax-advantaged bills provide various investment alternatives, allowing you to tailor your portfolio in your chance tolerance and financial desires.

Reduce danger: Diversification mitigates the effect of market volatility and protects your wealth over time.

- **Long-time period economic planning:**

Tax-advantaged bills inspire long-term saving: by way of locking away your cash for retirement or other lengthy-time period goals, you are much less likely to withdraw it upfront and derail your monetary plans.

Secure your economic destiny: those bills offer a dependable supply of income in retirement and let you attain monetary independence.

Here are some popular types of tax-advantaged accounts:

Retirement Accounts:

401(k): Employer-sponsored retirement account offering tax-deferred growth and potential employer matching contributions.

IRA: Individual retirement account with various contribution options and tax advantages, including traditional and Roth IRAs.

Education Savings Accounts:

529 College Savings Plan: Tax-advantaged account for saving for education expenses, offering tax-free growth and withdrawals for qualified educational costs.

Health Savings Accounts:

HSA: Account linked to a high-deductible health plan, offering tax-deductible contributions, tax-free growth, and tax-free withdrawals for qualified medical expenses.

Other Tax-Advantaged Accounts:

Archer MSA: Tax-advantaged account for individuals with qualified medical expenses not covered by health insurance.

Flexible Spending Account: Employer-sponsored account for paying for qualified medical or dependent care expenses, with tax-deductible contributions.

Here are some tips for utilizing tax-advantaged accounts effectively:

Start early: The earlier you start contributing, the more time your investments have to grow tax-deferred.

Contribute as much as possible: Maximize your contributions to take full advantage of the tax benefits.

Diversify your portfolio: Invest in various asset classes within your chosen account to reduce risk and enhance long-term returns.

Seek professional guidance: Consult a financial advisor for personalized advice on choosing the right accounts and implementing effective investment strategies.

Review your accounts regularly: Rebalance your portfolio periodically and adjust your contributions as needed to align with your evolving financial goals.

by using tax-advantaged bills strategically, you may significantly raise your wealth accumulation, minimize your tax burden, and relax a brighter monetary future for yourself and your loved ones. bear in thoughts, the ones debts constitute valuable gear for prolonged-term economic planning, and it is vital to understand their abilities, blessings, and limitations to maximize their effectiveness in achieving your dreams

Long-Term Financial Planning

lengthy-term economic making plans are the cornerstone of financial stability and success. It involves setting meaningful desires, crafting a comprehensive approach, and making disciplined selections to relax your economic destiny. here are 4 key outlines to manual your long-term economic planning:

1. Outline Your monetary goals:
- **Discover short-time period and long-term goals:**

Start by honestly defining your economic goals. Distinguish between short-time period dreams (e.g., growing an emergency fund, paying off high-hobby debt) and long-time period desires (e.g., homeownership, retirement).

- **Prioritize desires:**

Prioritize your goals based on their significance and timeline. This enables you to allocate resources and attention on reaching one purpose at a time at the same time as maintaining a broader angle.

- **Quantify and Time-bound desires:**

Quantify your desires in terms of unique quantities and set timeframes for fulfillment. As an instance, decide how much you need to shop for retirement and with the aid of what age you intend to retire.

2. Create a complete price range:
- **Song income and costs:**

develop an in depth budget that debts for all assets of earnings and categorizes charges. information your cash waft is important for effective monetary making plans.

- **Allocate budget to desires:**

Allocate a portion of your income to every economic goal. Prioritize requirements however make certain that your finances displays contributions to both brief-term and long-time period objectives.

- **Evaluate and adjust Periodically:**

often assess your price range and adjust it as needed. existence occasions, earnings changes, and sudden expenses may additionally necessitate modifications to make sure continued development toward your goals.

3. make investments for lengthy-term increase:

- **Set up a varied investment Portfolio:**

expand a properly-varied investment portfolio that aligns together with your threat tolerance, time horizon, and financial dreams. don't forget a mix of shares, bonds, and different properties to optimize long-time period increase capacity.

- **Take benefit of Tax-Advantaged accounts:**

utilize tax-advantaged bills like 401(k)s, IRAs, and HSAs to maximize the tax blessings associated with long-term investments. Contributions to those debts may also provide instantaneous tax blessings, and earnings can develop tax-deferred or tax-loose.

- **Rebalance and review frequently:**

Periodically evaluate your investment portfolio and rebalance it to maintain the favored asset allocation. existence adjustments, marketplace fluctuations, and evolving desires may additionally warrant modifications on your funding approach.

4. incorporate risk management techniques:

- **Make certain good enough insurance insurance:**

verify your insurance desires and ensure good enough insurance for lifestyles, health, incapacity, and belongings. Insurance acts as a financial protection net, protecting your belongings and loved ones from unexpected occasions.

- **Build and maintain Emergency budget:**

Establish an emergency fund to cover 3 to 6 months' worth of dwelling costs. This fund provides an economic cushion in case of unexpected task loss, scientific expenses, or other emergencies, preventing the need to build up debt.

- **Plan for Contingencies:**

Don't forget capability contingencies for your lengthy-term monetary plan. This includes elements like market downturns, financial recessions, or adjustments in private occasions. Having contingency plans enhances your economic resilience.

Retirement Planning

Retirement making plans entails determining retirement earnings desires and what's needed to acquire the ones dreams. Retirement planning includes identifying income assets, sizing up prices, imposing a savings application, and handling property and risk. future cash flows are expected to gauge whether or not the retirement income goal is possible.

you could start at any time, but it works great in case you element it into your economic making plans as early as viable. That's the best way to ensure a secure, cozy—and fun—retirement. The fun component is why it makes experience to take note of the critical and perhaps dull component: planning the way you'll get there.

How Retirement planning Works

Inside the best feeling, retirement making plans is what one does to be organized for lThe non-monetary elements encompass lifestyle selections along with how to spend time in retirement, wherein to stay, and while to give up working altogether, amongst different matters. A holistic method to retirement making plans considers some of these regions.

The emphasis that one puts on retirement planning adjustments at distinctive levels of existence. as an instance:

Early in a person's operating existence, retirement making plans is about putting aside sufficient money for retirement.

at some stage in the middle of your career, it'd additionally encompass placing particular earnings or asset targets and taking steps to acquire them.

Once you reach retirement age, you pass from collecting belongings to what planners call the distribution phase. You're not paying into your retirement account(s). As a substitute, your long time of financial savings begins paying you out.

life after paid paintings ends. This isn't simply financially however in all elements of life.

How good a deal Do You need to Retire?

remember the fact that retirement making plans starts lengthy earlier than you retire. The overall rule is the sooner you start, the better. Your magic wide variety, that's the quantity you want to retire easily, is fairly Customized. However there are numerous rules of thumb that can provide you with a concept of how a great deal.

How an awful lot you need depends on who you ask. as an example:

human beings used to mention that you want around $1 million to retire readily.

Different professionals use the eighty% rule, which states that you need sufficient to stay on 80% of your profits at retirement. So if you made $100,000 in step within 12 months, then you could need savings that could produce $80,000 in line with 12 months for roughly 20 years, or a complete of $1.6 million, along with the income generated by means of your retirement belongings.

Others say most retirees aren't saving anywhere close to enough to satisfy their benchmarks and must regulate their life-style to stay on what they have.

Even as the amount of money you will need to have in your nest egg is essential, it's also a great idea to not forget all your fees. make certain to calculate the costs for housing, medical insurance, food, clothing, and your car/transportation. And since you'll have more free time in your fingers, you could also want to component within the fee of leisure and tour. At the same time as it could be hard to come up with concrete figures, make certain to provide you with a reasonable estimate so there are no surprises in a while.

Begin as early as you may on whatever approach that you, and in all likelihood an economic planner, use to calculate your retirement financial savings wishes.

Steps to Retirement planning

Regardless of where you are in lifestyles, there are numerous key steps that practice to almost absolutely everyone throughout their retirement making plans.

The subsequent are some of the most not unusual:

provide you with a plan. This includes finding out when you want to start saving whilst you need to retire, and how much you want to shop for your remaining goal.

determine how a great deal you will set apart every month. Using automatic deductions takes away the guesswork, continues you on track, and takes away the temptation to stop or neglect depositing cash for your personal use.

pick the proper money owed for you. Take the risk to put money into a 401(ok) or similar account in case your enterprise offers that choice. Bear in mind, if the business enterprise gives an employer health and also you don't sign on, you are just giving away loose cash. And remember to have an emergency fund, which can be effortlessly liquidated in case you need cash in a pinch.

take a look at your investments occasionally and make periodic adjustments. It is usually an amazing concept to make any modifications every time there is a trade in your life-style and when you input a distinctive stage for your life.

Saving for Major Life Events

Life is full of twists and turns. From milestones to foremost existence selections, the price tag of change can shake up your budgeting method more than you'll suppose. Keeping a month-to-month finances takes diligence and continuous evaluation to stay on par along with your financial wishes. But, a recent ballot through Gallop determined that about 1/3 of American citizens (32%) preserve household finances.

without a strategic plan and price range in the area, you may face monetary fret while approached with predominant existence occasions. Be organized for existence's moments so that you can live centered on living them!

a way to finances for these 5 predominant existence events

- **New goals**

Whether or not you're saving to make a primary purchase like a new automobile or home or making plans for a lavish holiday, accommodating for a larger fee takes a toll on your universal spending and savings habits. treat your financial savings as a cost that you mechanically deduct out of each paycheck till you attain your aim. The usage of a budget binder assists you to identify where in your price range are being used and reveal how much cash you can set aside every month.

- **Getting Married**

In case you're tying the knot, be sure to tie up free leads to your price range. In 2018, the common wedding fee couples an stunning $33,931! With more and more couples footing the bill for his or her wedding ceremony instead of their families, it's first-rate to mention "I Do" to a wedding budget. dedicate some time to getting to know carriers and venues to your location and prioritize your spending on the aspects of your large day that genuinely matter. as an example, your venue can be your huge-price ticket object and you could cut returns at the prices of your décor. Or, you could decide you need an easier set-up the day of and allocate extra of your budget in the direction of your photographers to seize each second. placing strict limits on how much you need to spend for every factor of your wedding ceremony can guide you through the wedding making plans without spending a quiet penny.

First comes love, then comes marriage, then comes…. the "money speak". As a pair, you'll need to strategize how you'll together control your money and annual charges. A 2017 take a look at discovered that money is the primary trouble that married couples argue approximately. From shopping your weekly groceries to signing a loan, selecting finances is a crucial piece of merging price range as a pair.

- **Changing Jobs**

When converting jobs, you'll want to restructure your finances to coincide on your new profits and pay schedule. If your new role is slated to pay you greater than your preceding business enterprise, you might want to not forget to allocate your extra funds immediately into a savings account. This enhancement for your financial institution account has to prompt you to revisit your budgeting approach to correspond together with your new income and any added charges which could rise up (which includes a longer go back and forth, new garments in your position, and so on).

you will also need to not forget any adjustments on your pay schedule in evaluation with when your month-to-month bills are due as it can have an effect on the way you distribute and finances your profits. take into account that your final paycheck from your preceding organization and your first paycheck out of your new job will fall. relying on this time frame, you can want to be a little greater frugal about your spending to keep you over till you receive your new pay.

Other elements to keep in mind when switching jobs is whether or not you may receive a payout from your vacation/unwell days and what you'll do together with your retirement plan once you go away. Weigh your options and speak with an experienced professional to determine what path of motion is satisfactory for you.

- **Starting your own family**

beginning a family is, no longer only, a prime life trade but a first-rate finances changer as well. The common price of elevating a child has risen to $233,610 for a middle-class family of two youngsters. garb, baby components, toys, vehicle seats, and gadget, are only some of the expenses that need to be blanketed whilst adding toddlers to the mix. As your child grows so will the amounts and obligations. As soon as your infant reaches college age, your price range might also want to fluctuate to consist of recreational activities and entertainment, childcare, school elements and so on. There are some approaches to staying budget-savvy as a circle of relatives that, when combined with a wholesome budget, can keep you on track with assembling your financial savings dreams.

Growing your circle of relatives will even notably have an effect on some of your economic practices, which includes; insurance and fitness care fees, filing your taxes, and adjustments to your existence insurance wishes. You will also need to not forget contributing to a college financial savings plan, such as a 529 plan, to help shield and at ease your baby(ren's) destiny. Duncan economic organization gives education planning services to estimate and put together for the fees of better training. talk with an advisor to learn more!

- **Retirement**

Whether you're just joining the workforce or if retirement is on the horizon, it's essential that you check your retirement plan and lay out a budget that is relaxed to your way of life and needs. the sooner you start saving- the higher! Running with a monetary consultant allows you to strategically store to make ends meet at some stage in retirement. you'll want to estimate your annual prices, fitness care prices, and any goals (visiting, relocating, hobbies, etc) you need to deal with your average price range.

Some individuals pick to work component-time at some stage in retirement to gather supplemental earnings similar to social safety or your 401(okay) funds. Having a protection cushion to fall again on can assist cover any unexpected fees that could stand up, and alleviate a number of the budgetary worries that many face during retirement.

The Simple Guide To Budgeting

Conclusion

Recap of Key Principles

Embarking on a journey toward financial success involves understanding and applying key principles that guide your decisions and actions. Let's recap the fundamental principles covered across various aspects of personal finance:

Balance Is Key
Overview
    Achieving financial balance entails managing various aspects of your financial life, including income, expenses, savings, and investments, to create a harmonious and sustainable financial plan.

Key Components
    Prioritize balance in income vs. expenses, short-term vs. long-term goals, and spending vs. saving to build a robust financial foundation.

Budgeting Checklist
Budgeting is a cornerstone of economic success. A budgeting checklist helps structure your financial plan, ensuring you cover essential elements and allocate resources effectively.

Components
    Create a comprehensive budget that includes income assessment, tracking expenses, emergency funds, and strategic spending to align your financial habits with your goals.

Investing:

Investing is a vital element of wealth building. Understanding different investment vehicles, risk management, and incorporating investments into your budget contributes to long-term financial success.

Components

Diversify your portfolio, consider tax implications, set realistic goals, and periodically review and adjust your investment strategy to align with your financial objectives.

Understanding Tax Implications

Overview

Understanding the tax implications of investments and utilizing tax-advantaged accounts are essential for optimizing your after-tax returns and maximizing the benefits of various investment vehicles.

Components

Differentiate between taxable and tax-advantaged accounts, consider capital gains and losses, explore tax-efficient investments, and strategically utilize tax-advantaged accounts.

Long-Term Financial Planning

Overview:

Long-term financial planning involves setting clear goals, creating a comprehensive budget, investing strategically, and incorporating risk management strategies to build a solid financial foundation for the future.

Components

Define financial goals, create a budget, invest for growth, incorporate risk management, regularly review and adjust your plan, and seek professional advice for personalized guidance.

Retirement Planning

Retirement planning is a dynamic process that requires setting clear goals, calculating savings needs, creating a diversified portfolio, and implementing a sustainable withdrawal strategy for a secure retirement.

Components

Set clear retirement goals, calculate savings needs, create a diversified portfolio, maximize retirement savings contributions, factor in healthcare costs, implement a sustainable withdrawal strategy, stay informed about tax planning, and periodically review and adjust your plan.

Saving for Major Life Events

Saving for major life events involves identifying and prioritizing goals, creating specific savings buckets, choosing appropriate savings vehicles, budgeting effectively, utilizing windfalls, exploring assistance, and regularly monitoring progress.

Components:

Identify and prioritize life events, create specific savings buckets, choose appropriate savings vehicles, budget and allocate resources, utilize windfalls and bonuses, explore assistance and discounts, regularly monitor progress, and celebrate milestones and achievements.

Incorporating those key ideas into your economic method empowers you to make knowledgeable selections, adapt to converting circumstances, and in the long run reap your monetary goals. by retaining a holistic and balanced approach to non-public finance, you lay the foundation for a hit and pleasurable monetary adventure.

Encouragement for Continued Financial Success

Embarking on an adventure in the direction of economic achievement is a sizable success, and as you navigate this route, it is important to live motivated and resilient. here are phrases of encouragement to encourage you to continue your pursuit of monetary properly-being:

Have a good timing on Your progress
Every step you're taking, regardless of how small, is a victory. celebrate your achievements and milestones alongside the manner. spotting your development boosts morale and fuels your motivation to keep shifting ahead.

Embrace lifelong learning
The world of private finance is dynamic and ever-evolving. embrace a mind-set of lifelong learning. live curious, explore new monetary strategies, and adapt to converting situations. expertise is an effective tool on your journey.

Examine from challenges
demanding situations are a natural part of any monetary adventure. in place of seeing them as setbacks, view demanding situations as possibilities to learn and grow. Every impediment you overcome strengthens your resilience and equips you with precious revel in.

Outline Your Why
Reconnect with the motives behind your monetary goals. Whether it is supplying protection in your family, pursuing a passion, or taking part in a comfortable retirement, information about your "why" adds motive on your economic journey and continues to encourage you.

Stay consistent

Consistency is key in reaching lasting economic achievement. stay devoted to your price range, savings plan, and funding approach. Small, consistent efforts over time yield significant outcomes.

Be patient and continual

Economic fulfillment is a journey that unfolds over the years. Be patient with the manner and continual effort. understand that your financial goals are worth the time and willpower you put money into.

Celebrate Non-monetary Wins

monetary achievement extends beyond numbers. have a good time non-monetary wins, which include building healthful financial habits, fostering subjects, and making informed decisions. These features are useful for your adventure.

Surround yourself with aid

constructing a robust assist system is critical. surround yourself with those who proportion your financial values or are supportive of your desires. A supportive network offers encouragement at some stage in tough times.

Visualize Your future

Take time to visualize the future you're working in the direction of. Whether or not it's picturing a debt-unfastened life, a dream excursion, or an at ease retirement, visualization reinforces your dedication and fuels your willpower.

Exercise Self-Compassion

economic journeys are full of u.s.a.and downs. Be type to yourself during hard moments. understand that setbacks are opportunities for growth, and self-compassion is an effective motivator.

Encourage Others

 proportion your economic journey and successes with others. inspire the ones around you to embark on their own paths in the direction of economic nicely-being. The fine impact you've got on others can be a worthwhile element of your adventure.

consider, economic achievement is not a destination but a non-stop adventure. By means of staying superb, mastering from experiences, and preserving a ahead-looking attitude, you're laying the muse for a destiny full of monetary property-being and achievement. preserve going, and understand that every effort you invest these days contributes to a brighter future.

Resources for Ongoing Learning

Continued learning is a key thing of economic achievement, and thankfully, there are various sources to be had that will help you live knowledgeable and empowered to your journey. here are various sorts of resources you can explore for ongoing monetary education:

Books:
"The Total Money Makeover" by Dave Ramsey: offers sensible recommendations on budgeting, debt reduction, and building wealth.
"Your money or Your life" with the aid of Vicki Robin and Joe Dominguez: Explores the relationship between cash and existence pleasure, emphasizing the importance of mindful spending and saving.

Podcasts:
The Dave Ramsey display: presents sensible financial recommendations on budgeting, debt control, and building wealth.
The Clark Howard Podcast: Covers a wide range of private finance subjects, from saving cash on normal charges to investing.

Online courses:
Khan Academy personal finance: offers loose on-line courses overlaying diverse private finance topics, including budgeting, investing, and retirement planning.
Coursera - financial planning for teens: A route that covers crucial monetary planning ideas for teenagers.

Websites and Blogs:
Investopedia: an intensive online useful resource for economic schooling, providing articles, tutorials, and educational content material on numerous financial subjects.
NerdWallet: gives guides and equipment to assist with budgeting, investing, and choosing the right economic products.

YouTube Channels:
Graham Stephan: An actual property investor and private finance YouTuber who stocks realistic advice on building wealth and accomplishing economic fulfillment.
The financial diet: Covers a huge range of personal finance subjects, together with budgeting, saving, and making an investment, with a focal point on a holistic method to monetary well-being.

Monetary Apps:
Mint: A budgeting app that tracks your spending, enables you to set economic goals, and offers insights into your economic behavior.
Acorns: An app that rounds up your regular purchases to make investments in the spare trade, making investing easy and automatic.

Newsletters:
Morning Brew: A daily newsletter protecting financial information and trends in a concise and engaging layout.
The Motley fool: offers newsletters with investment insights, inventory pointers, and educational content.

Financial Advisors and Planners:
seeking recommendation from certified financial planners or advisors can offer customized steering based on your particular economic situation and goals.

Webinars and Seminars:
Many financial establishments and educational structures host webinars and seminars on numerous monetary subjects. check with nearby community facilities, economic institutions, or online platforms for upcoming activities.

Network resources:
neighborhood community centers, libraries, and person training programs regularly provide monetary literacy workshops and seminars. Those sources can offer treasured insights and networking opportunities.

don't forget, the important thing to ongoing learning is to explore a spread of assets that align together with your mastering style and options. Whether or not you opt for studying books, listening to podcasts, participating in online publications, or engaging with monetary experts, there is a wealth of knowledge available that will help you in your adventure to monetary achievement.

www.ingramcontent.com/pod-product-compliance
Lightning Source LLC
Chambersburg PA
CBHW062321290526
45794CB00005B/1849